Hope Whispers

Edited By Lynn C. Johnston

Whispering Angel Books

A Whispering Angel Book

Hope Whispers

ISBN 978-0-9841421-0-1

0-9841421-0-X

Whispering Angel Books

2416 W. Victory Blvd #234

Burbank, CA 91506

http://www.whisperingangelbooks.com

Printed in the United States of America

Whispering Angel Books is dedicated to publishing uplifting and inspirational works for its readers while donating a portion of its book sales to charitable organizations promoting physical, emotional and spiritual healing. If you'd like to learn more about our books or our fundraising programs for your charity, please visit our website: www.whisperingangelbooks.com

"When the world says, 'give up'
hope whispers, 'try it one more time.' "

~ Unknown

Contents

DEDICATION

This book is dedicated to the memory of Mimi, Cecil, Grace and Wendy. Without their influence, this book would not have been possible.

ACKNOWLEDGMENTS

The creation and development of this book would not have been possible without the assistance of many people. I would like to thank everyone who submitted their heartfelt stories and poems for this anthology. With hundreds of wonderful pieces to choose from, each prospective contributor made the selection process far more challenging and rewarding than imaginable.

My deepest appreciation goes out to Ed Johnston, Julie G. Beers, Frannie Mathews and Elaine Voss for sharing their expertise, opinions and support during this process.

INTRODUCTION

Hope is... an outstretched hand in the dark... a staircase into the unknown... a thing with feathers that perches in our soul. Poets, philosophers and spiritual leaders have always used a myriad of images to describe our intangible belief that things will improve – the illness will be cured, love will be found and the dream will be achieved.

Hope, which is often an extension of faith, can be inspired by God or religious scripture. Sometimes it's found in the compassion of a stranger lending a hand after a disaster – and sometimes hope whispers into the deepest recesses of our spirit fortifying our own determination to succeed. Even in the worst of times, we can still find a reason to hope.

I learned that lesson from my maternal grandmother. Mimi, as she was nicknamed, was an amazing woman. She was loving and compassionate – and she spoiled me every chance she got. I was her first grandchild, and I would end up being the only granddaughter, which made me even more special in her eyes. According to Mimi, I could do no wrong. She always said that if I ever killed someone, she knew I'd have a good reason. Fortunately, I never had to prove it.

When I was little, Mimi was a frequent visitor in our home. Several days a week, she would arrive for afternoon coffee with my mother. They'd give me a ceramic mug of milk with a splash of coffee in it, so I wouldn't feel left out. Mimi always took the time to make sure I was included in the conversation.

Being with her was always a treat for me. Our time together was often spent playing or singing. If she wasn't teaching me the words to "Lavender Blue" or another children's song, it would be a current hit by one of our favorite performers like Dionne Warwick or The Carpenters.

Sometimes, we just watched TV together. I have vivid memories of sitting on her lap at three years old watching "The Wizard of Oz" for the first time. Frightened by the flying monkeys and the wicked witch, I clung to her as her soothing voice reassured me of my safety. Looking back, I'm grateful it was a black-and-white TV. Had I known that the Wicked Witch of the West was green back then, I may have never left her lap.

In the end, it really didn't matter what Mimi and I were doing because it was being together that always made it special.

As we both grew older, things changed a bit. I went on to college and moved across the country to California. Months apart turned into years, but we always kept in touch. Then she became a great-grandmother when I gave birth to my son, Sam.

It was something she could hardly comprehend: partly because she couldn't believe her "little" 30-year-old granddaughter was now a mother herself; the other part was due to the early stages of dementia.

Like Alzheimer's, dementia is a cruel disease. It takes wonderfully vital, competent and intelligent people and strips them of their mental capacities, including their lifetime of memories.

When she started telling people in her nursing home that I was her niece – and that my son was my mother's child, I knew the woman I loved all my life was quickly disappearing. I also knew that the wonderful memories we once shared together were now mine alone.

I had always been a firm believer that we ultimately get what we deserve: good or bad. I think that's what made her condition so devastating for me. She certainly never deserved this. I thought how cruel it was of God to inflict this disease on her. How could He let this happen to such an incredible woman? It was a strong blow to my faith, which was already on shaky ground from some of life's other disappointments. And when she passed away on that August morning, I knew my life would never be the same.

That night I sat dazed in my apartment staring at the television, channel surfing mindlessly. When I came across a biography of "The Carpenters," I paused momentarily.

Within a few seconds, their song, "They Long to Be (Close to You)" starting playing. It snapped me out of my daze and, for the first time that day, a smile burst from my lips.

It was our song… and I had almost completely forgotten about it. Mimi used to say the song was all about me. She would sit me on her lap, wrap her arms around me and we'd sway back and forth while she sang.

As I listened to those words flow from Karen Carpenter, I knew it was Mimi's sign to me that she had crossed over successfully. The woman I knew and loved was back. What had been taken from her in the cruelest of ways had been restored on the other side.

At that point, I started to realize that no matter how bad things seem, no situation is ever really hopeless. When we least expect it, hope can be resurrected. And if we listen closely, we may discover that hope can still be heard – sometimes hope speaks, sometimes it sings and sometimes hope whispers.

BACK FROM THE BRINK
By Cherise Wyneken

Leave his bag in your car," the registrar told us, "until you know which room he'll be assigned to."

My husband was entering the hospital for a standard surgical procedure. It was expected to take a couple of hours and require no more than a two night stay.

I kissed him good-bye at the entrance for a surgery at 5:30, Thursday morning. The attendant directed me to wait in the family room of the outpatient division where I ran into a woman from our neighborhood. We exchanged our reasons for being there – surgeries for her son and for my husband.

The day wore on and on and still no word. I was glad for my neighbor's presence and her help in passing the time, but my concern was growing. What happened? What went wrong? At last I approached the volunteer. She called surgery and was told I should expect a several hour delay. By that time my neighbor's son was released. "I'll pray for your husband," she said as she waved good-bye.

Pray. Yes. That's what I need to do, I thought. *But maybe he wouldn't want me to.* I was thinking of all those heated discussions we had had concerning prayer. I was a long time believer that God often gives us what we ask for. Perhaps – just because we acknowledge him and ask. My husband disagreed. "What about those other people who pray and don't get what they ask for?" he would counter. I was well aware that it wasn't magic. It had been my experience that sometimes God says yes; sometimes he says no – but gives us grace to cope. And sometimes he says wait. My husband's words had set me wondering, but I began to pray.

Late that afternoon the doctors finally appeared with their report, wearing weary, worried looks. Once they'd gotten inside his

1

body, they found a nest of complications. My husband was critically ill. His lungs were damaged and he needed to be on a respirator. "He'll have to stay in recovery for a while," they said. "Then we'll send him to the Critical Care Unit and let you know when you can see him."

So I waited and prayed some more. It was time now, too, for the volunteer at the desk to go home. She instructed me to stay there and answer her phone when they called. Time went on and on until I became frantic. I found my way to CCU and entered – without the regulation tag. When a young male nurse approached and asked how he could help, I burst into tears. "I said goodbye to my husband early this morning and I don't know where he is or how he is." He graciously sat me down and after some phone calls, informed me that my husband would be there soon.

As I waited in the nearby family room, I finally saw that beloved face being wheeled through the corridor. After getting him settled, they called me in – warning me to prepare for a shock. Tubes were in his nose and mouth, a respirator pulsed nearby, drainage tubes were connected to plastic containers lining the wall behind him, a screen beeped, flashing signs of his vitals. I was overwhelmed and asked if I could stay the night. They were very kind, but said, "No."

That was bad enough, but by the next weekend I watched the nurse struggle to bring up his vital signs. The doctor was called in and told me, "He has multi-system organ failure. His only hope is another operation, but I doubt he can make it through alive." His words struck like a lightning bolt – leaving a big black hole in my heart. *No! No! I don't want to lose him yet*, I screamed inside. After fifty-three years of marriage one begins to take a relationship for granted, but that night I knew without a doubt, how much I still wanted him with me.

I called our children – 3,000 miles away – and prayed. Our friend, Jon, came and stood by me as they prepared for the operation. "With all these machines and tubes, I can't even reach to kiss him good-bye," I said.

"Don't worry," the nurse said. "We'll fix it so you can."

When everything had been unplugged from the wall and realigned into a battery at the foot of the bed, we were able to reach him. Jon took my husband's hand and told him he'd never had such a wonderful friend. I kissed him once for each of our four children, naming them as I did. Then I kissed him from myself – thanking him for being such a good husband. There was no sign that he had heard. I went to the family room sobbing uncontrollably. When the doctor came with his report, the smile on his face told us there was hope.

I notified my husband's siblings and friends. Our children came and, even the scoffers among them prayed. The ensuing week added the dialysis machine to his plastic life. At least he was still living and we

2

had hope. That was until the weekend rolled around again, bringing news that the sack around his heart was filling with fluid. There would be another surgery – another life threatening situation – from which they didn't expect him to survive.

Everyone who heard about it prayed for him: the maid who cleaned his room, the nurses and the doctors, our family and friends, the people who waited in the family room for news of their own loved ones, the pastor who came to call and the nuns as they made their rounds. As they rolled the gurney down the hall toward surgery, I ran up asking if I could kiss him. "We don't have time," they called as they rushed on.

But once again I saw the gurney return with my husband's living body. While they had him out on the operating table, they performed a tracheotomy so the tubes could be removed from his mouth and oxygen could be transmitted through the opening in his throat. At least he was more comfortable.

"How is your husband?" people asked. "We're praying for him."

I assumed they were praying that he'd get well. But it seemed that every time we thought he was recovering, some major setback appeared. At last – instead of asking God to heal him – I put it in his hands. "Dear God," I said. "I don't know which way to pray – what to ask for. You know all things, so you know he wouldn't want to be kept alive on machines. Please do what you think best and help me cope."

Slowly his condition improved. The dialysis machine was put aside, the oxygen supply was weaned, tubes were taken out and the needles were removed. After six weeks he was moved to Intermediate Care and then to Rehab. Two months from the day I took him there, I brought him home. A man alive.

TALISMAN
By Sharon Scholl

"I will come back,"
he says. "I will let you know
somehow." He grips
his side where cancer
spreads its roots like Chinese
tallows, sprouts fistulas
like palm seed pods.

He will be a bird, he swears:
egret, whooping crane, something
large and white, gleaming
like an affirmation.

With the funeral and all
we forget his solemn oath
until on the grimy floor
of the office elevator -
one long white feather.

THE EAGLE HAS LANDED
By Edward Louis

"The Eagle has landed," I said confidently into the lobby telephone of a quiet Rio de Janeiro hotel. As I hung up, the desk clerk looked at me oddly.

"Just calling my wife," I nodded and began dragging my suitcase towards the elevator.

It was my safe arrival call back home – the importance of which had been drilled into me by my father as I was growing up.

It seemed I couldn't leave our property without hearing him bellow, "Call me when you get there." His desire to protect us was ever-present. "Watch where you're going" or "be careful with that" tripped off his tongue as easily as "hello."

As I grew up, got married and started my own family, I began to understand his need to know that nothing had harmed us when we were away from him. Life was good, but my job required me to do a lot of international traveling. Long flights, busy meetings and hotel rooms in foreign countries meant little time for me to watch over my family – or for my family to watch over me.

Before the advent of cell phones and email, personal communication from these locales was often inconvenient and always expensive. Instead of having a long telephone conversation relaying the day's events, a brief "safe arrival" call would have to suffice. I would call my wife, Wendy, and recite the famous words said by Neil Armstrong in 1969 during the Apollo 11 moon landing: "The Eagle has landed." With that simple phrase, she would know that I had gotten to my destination as planned and everything was okay.

As our kids grew up and moved away, she, too, would have her share of exotic travels – like to California to see our daughter or to Florida to visit our sons. No matter where she went, I could be assured of a safe arrival call with our signature phrase.

5

Over the years, we discussed the last trip either one of us would ever have to take – that trip to the "Great Beyond." We always said that the one who got there first needed to send back a sign that they had crossed over successfully – in essence, giving a "safe arrival" call.

More than 30 years later – and eight months after being diagnosed with pancreatic cancer – my wife took that final trip. The thought of any kind of sign was the furthest thing from my mind. But on the morning of her funeral, my sister and I spotted an eagle flying over our house.

It might not have been such a big deal if eagles were commonly seen in my area, but they aren't. It was the first – and last – time I had ever seen one in several years of living there. My next door neighbor, who is an avid bird watcher, also saw the eagle that morning and confirmed it was a rare sighting.

The eagle circled our home and perched itself in a large tree on our property. It stared down at us for the longest time – almost as if it wanted to make sure we saw it.

"It's Wendy," my sister announced as we stared back at the eagle. Tears began to fill my eyes as we watched it finally fly away. "I think you're right. It's her sign to us: the eagle has landed."

MY OLD LOVABLE NEW FRIEND
By Susan Berg

A funny thing happened to me just the other day.
The friendliest cat came to my door wanting to play.
He was meowing like crazy, peering in through the screen,
As if calling to someone it'd been a while since he'd seen.

I said, "Well, hello little kitty. What is it you want?
I've never seen you before. Are you just out for a jaunt?"
He was an orange and white Tabby with a depth in his eyes.
Of all the cats I've known, he was the most lovable guy.

As I petted him gently, he met my every touch.
He loved all the attention and just couldn't get enough.
I gave him some ham scraps and some water to drink.
He gobbled it all up; then was gone in a blink.

A few days went by when one night I couldn't sleep.
I stepped outside beneath the lamppost on our street.
I looked up at the stars as I so often do,
And talked to God and loved ones who are up there, too.

I thought I'd sure like to see that cute, friendly cat.
And right at that moment, he appeared! Just like that!
He came out from underneath the cars in our drive
And walked right to me. I couldn't believe my eyes!

We were both so overjoyed as if long lost friends
Who were finally able to embrace once again.
He squirmed with such delight at my every stroke.
In his eyes, I saw my friend Teddy — that's no joke.

You see, Teddy was my life-long friend who sadly died.
I miss him every day and often look for "a sign."
I asked the cat, "Are you Teddy?" Our eyes locked in a gaze.
Just then, as if answering, he raised one paw to my face.

He reached up with his paw and gently touched my chin.
It gave me goose bumps because I just knew it was him!
In awe, it took me a few minutes to take this all in.
Then, I said goodbye to my friend, "Hope to see you again."

The next morning in the yard he played wild and carefree.
He was running and jumping and climbing a tree.
That's the last time I saw him— don't know where he could be,
Or whom he belongs to, but I sure wish it was me!

I wonder, was it Teddy visiting me as a cat?
Maybe, just maybe? I'd like to think it was fact.
I'd sure love to see "my old lovable new friend,"
But, seems he's vanished—I haven't seen him since then.

If my friend ever does pay me a visit again,
I think I might keep him, if it is all right with him.

This poem is a true story about a wonderful, yet mysterious encounter I had with a most lovable cat that briefly visited me in 2003 right after my life-long friend, Teddy Lopez, sadly died at the young age of 42.

BELLS AND WHISTLES
By Kathleen Gerard

My mother and I had traveled from New Jersey and arrived in Baltimore on the eve of my seventh foot surgery. I couldn't sleep, so I took another bath. I basked in this luxury, as I knew I'd be trapped in another fiberglass cast and wouldn't be able to bathe my whole body for at least three months.

When I stepped from the tub, I caught an image of myself in the full-length mirror hung on the back of the bathroom door. Balancing on my cane, I let my towel drop to the floor and stood naked and barefoot before my own reflected image. Scars riddled my body like fossils. Six years of surgery were reflected in my thighs, where tourniquets had been tightened; and in my hips, where bone had been excised for grafts. And my feet – every side, except the soles – were marked from six other failed operations to correct degenerating soft tissue and bone.

It was hard to believe this was the body of a twenty-four year-old woman – a woman who used to play tennis for hours and take long walks on the beach. Now my posture was crooked and there was only anguish reflecting back from my face. "God," I whispered, "do you really want me to go through this all over again?"

Doubts about another operation surged and threatened to overtake my faith and positive affirmations. When doctors in the New York-Metropolitan area were leery to try again to "fix me," my mother suggested we visit a world-renowned hospital in Baltimore, Maryland. The doctors there spelled out all the risks, but they were hopeful and confident that they could help me get back on my feet. At first, I was energized by their optimism and was willing to undergo another operation. But with surgery less than twelve hours away, my mind was laden with fear and questions. Was I making the right choice – by trying again? Could I endure the pain? Keep off my feet for another three months to ensure that the bones would finally fuse and the tendons hold?   What if the surgery failed again?   What if there were complications? How would I deal with that – physically and emotionally? But what if this surgery was finally able to heal me?

Later, before I went to bed, I spewed my concerns to my mother.

"I know you're scared, Kath. But between now and the time you enter the operating room tomorrow," she suggested, "why not ask God to give you a confirmation - that by having another surgery, you are following His will for your life."

I've always marveled at my mother's belief that we are not human beings having a spiritual experience, but rather we are spiritual beings having a human experience. And I've been further in awe at how she lives her life accordingly, staying close to God in worship and prayer and expecting to hear from Him - as you would from a dear, trusted friend. I wished I possessed that kind of faith.

That night, in our hotel room 250 miles from home, I tossed and turned. The only way I was able to quiet my mind was to focus on the positive implications of my mother's wisdom.

"Okay, God," I prayed in my thoughts. "Help! Please give me a confirmation that I've made the right decision to have this next surgery and that healing is possible. I mean, it doesn't have to be bells and whistles - just something to show that you're in this with me, that I'm headed in the right direction . . ."

I turned over my pillow to the cool side for about the hundredth time, and I concentrated my thoughts on God and my prayer. I was finally drifting off to sleep, when, out from in the darkness, I suddenly heard a *thud!*

My body flinched. I was jolted awake. As I sat up and turned on the light, I discovered that my leg braces had somehow fallen off the dresser and had landed upon the floor. My mother, who was in the adjacent bed, slept through the fleeting disturbance, but this was confirmation enough for me.

"Thanks, God," I whispered in gratitude and turned off the light. I could feel the corners of my mouth curl as I looked up into the dark ceiling and made the sign of the cross.

It was two hours later that my sleep was again disturbed. I woke to the sound of a torrential, violent thunderstorm with cracks of thunder and flashes of lightning that rattled the plate glass windows of the high-rise hotel. I got up from bed and peered through the drapes. Rain was coming down in sheets. Sirens were wailing through the vacant, yet now drenched city streets and blurry swirls of red and blue lights flashed, penetrating the darkness.

"I guess you're seeing to it that I got your message loud and clear, eh?" My whisper drifted into the dark, night sky, where the

10

heavens were wide open and showering down bells and whistles, after all.

When I woke early the next morning, I said to my mother, "I got my confirmation. Did you hear the intensity of that rain storm last night?"

"Rain? Did it rain?" she asked.

My eyes were wide. "Did it rain? Did it ever!" I pulled back the drapes to show her.

"Well, I guess there are a few puddles down there," she remarked, peering toward the street.

"A few puddles? But there was a downpour. You didn't hear it?"

A shrug was my mother's response.

"You mean, you didn't hear that thunder – and all those sirens?"

My mother swung her head from left to right. "Slept like a rock," she told me.

Did I imagine all that?

The first thing the doctor said when he greeted us at the hospital that morning was, "Did you both hear that rain last night? It was awesome – even blew out a transformer in the city. The weatherman says we got two inches in an hour . . ."

I looked at my mother, and we both beamed smiles at each other. I knew I'd gotten the confirmation I'd asked for – and then some. As I was wheeled away to the operating room, a sense of peace covered me like a warm blanket. In my heart I was convinced that, no matter what the outcome, I was exactly where I was supposed to be.

HEART
By Sarah Ward Merritt

Capture my heart and do not ever let go,
Let the wind carry me in its arms deep,
As the burdens of my heart wrestle slow,
Never will I forget dark nights of sleep.

Endless still mornings of quiet toil,
Will the sunlight kindle my smile today,
Shine my eyes sparkles of a soul loyal,
Replacing thoughts that would not go away.

Is it safe to dream of peace from above,
An ark for my hopes, dreams, thoughts and fears,
What will rescue me from pain is God's love,
Hedging me in for the rest of my years.

Believing the worst is far behind me,
I follow my heart speaking silently.

SOUL IN PERIL
By Barbara Watkins

Be it deep in the night or by sunlight of day,
my lost soul weighs heavy against my heart.
I look down the path to where I must journey.
It is a never ending circle lost with no beginning.
Desperate to break free my spirit soars high,
only to be beaten down from its inner demons.
To stay in this doom would surely mean death.
I must hasten to free my fears before the last hours.

I CAN HANDLE THEM ALL
By Gary W. Fort

All the cares and worries
I have carried around so long
God lifted them from my shoulders
And filled my heart with song
Though problems were overwhelming
Suddenly seem so small
Starting each day with prayer
I can handle them all.

WHATEVER, LORD
By Glenda Barrett

"Lean all the way back into the water, and you'll be able to float," my friend instructed me, as she attempted to teach me to swim. I remember trying several times before I could get the courage to do what she told me. It was so much harder than it looked. As I attempted to lean back, my ears filled with water and the struggle would begin. I fought the water to regain my standing position. With a lot of determination and persistence, I finally learned the secret: to relax and let go. It was then and only then, that I learned to float.

As I thought about this incident, it was so easy to compare it to my life today. Many losses I have suffered during the last ten years. During this period of time, I have been diagnosed with an incurable neuromuscular disease, had a spinal fusion, four foot surgeries, lost several family members to death and watched a child battling an alcohol problem.

This is not to mention the strain on my thirty year marriage due to all the stress and financial worries. More than one time, I felt so stressed I wanted to leave, to go anywhere to get away from all the pain. Instead, all I could do was to hang on for dear life.

Having been a Christian for many years, I learned to pray a different kind of prayer; not one with long fancy words, but one straight from the heart. In the middle of the night, while enduring endless muscle pain, I cried more than once, "Lord, I really need you!" To my amazement, I received a peace just like the Bible talks about, "the peace that passes all understanding."

It did not take me long to see if I didn't focus solely on God, I really wouldn't survive. There was not one area of my life I could look at that wasn't painful. I finally saw I'd have to start over and rebuild my life, much like beginning anew after a war.

As an independent woman, it was hard for me to ask, but I began to reach out for support - and I found I was not alone. After

14

working through the deep stages of grief, I began to look at what I had left, instead of what I had lost. Having been an artist from a child, I began to focus on my oil painting.

Also, I began to write deeply and personally straight from the heart, sometimes cutting it into shreds afterward. I began to yearn for meaningful relationships, so I began rebuilding old relationships and began making new friends, people that were positive and inspiring. Instead of complaining, I became more grateful and focused on every day being a day of gratitude.

Today, as I folded clothes that had been washed and dried, it occurred to me, "What a wonderful thing to be able to care for myself." Even as I ride through the grocery store on my scooter, I have smile on my face because it is a pleasure for me to grocery shop. In the past, before my illness, I would have moaned and groaned about doing housework and grocery shopping, thinking it was boring. What a difference a new perspective can make!

As I'm typing this, I am in my office surrounded by my special gifts accumulated over the years. Outside my window is a bird nest and feeder, where the birds swoop down and rest a bit before taking a sunflower seed and going their way, never seeming to mind the sound of Beethoven filling the air inside my room. Directly above the computer, I have a small quote saying, "Press on: Nothing in the world can take the place of persistence" – by Calvin Coolidge, along with a few other positive quotes. This room is my own special sanctuary; a place I can come to work in peace and harmony.

Today, my situation has not changed a lot, but the miracle of it all is that I've changed. It was only yesterday that someone asked me how I was doing and I replied, "Even though it has been difficult, these last three years have been the most meaningful of my life!"

I noticed the quizzical look he gave me; but I attempted to explain, "You see, it is almost like I have been reimbursed. Having gone through these difficult circumstances has taught me some valuable lessons. When you are really not sure how long you'll be able to do these things in life, they become even more precious. By learning to rely on God, I came to know Him on a deep personal level, much different than before. I have learned even though I cannot change my circumstances, I can control my attitude and hold dear to the joy He gives me. I have found beauty in stillness and a simple life, and I have discovered my true self."

What better way to live! Not only that, my first poetry chapbook was published last year, and my artwork is selling on an online gallery. How lucky I am to be able to do the things that I've always done as a child.

Much like my learning to swim, I had to learn to let go, cease the struggle and let God have control of my life. Now that I am relaxed and He is in charge of my life, I can float along smoothly. I would not be honest if I told you all this came easily or quickly. That was not the case. It only came when I was finally able to accept the situation and say in all earnest, "Whatever, Lord."

HOPES ON HIGH
By Karen M Miner

This cancer can erode my mortal life,
spread through my blood "metastically."
I'm not so foolish as to welcome strife
but this is not an ending that I see.

Though chemicals and radiation sear
and nausea haunts me long into the night.
My soul remains undaunted by the fear,
my vision drifts beyond this earthly plight.

If Christ lays healing hands I will remain,
perchance this is a fight for me to win.
Still I am certain that beyond all pain,
there is a light that leads me straight to Him!

BRIGID'S FORGE II
By Jean L. McCorkle-Kaess

Heated in the fires
Of Brigid's forge
I have been tested
And I have survived

Her fires I tend
Her heat sizzles
Ice of a freezer burned heart
I have been tested
And I survived

Stitching a steaming
Survival out of ice
I have been tested
And I have survived

Her hearth surrounded by
Hedge no man may pass
My ice, her hearth
Give them life
And they survive

Her eloquence speaks
Through my small words
Her blessings are many
Wisdom bright
I have been tested
And allowed to survive
Metal strengthened
In the fire of memory

I am tested
And I survive

She has healed me
Through her exquisite craft
As her smiths test
Metal in her forge
So she has tested me
And, in doing so
Given me strength to
Meet each sunrise
And always, always to survive

WAR STORY
By Susan Mahan

When death rifled my dreams
I put my heart on reserve
and marched resolutely in place

The plan of attack: nothing mattered
Life was neither good nor bad enough
to hold impenetrable despair at bay

I hid beneath a smoke screen, held on for dear life
and waited for hope to rescue my soul

Good news from the front: the reinforcements have arrived

MY GOD HUG
By William Creed

I lost my mind when I was thirty-seven. It didn't take long – less than a heart beat.

I was shaving when, without warning, I simply lost my mind. Suddenly, I didn't know where I was. I couldn't add or subtract, I didn't know what year it was, the names of my children or how old I was. I couldn't count to ten or even understand the English language, except for small words.

Lastly, I was now partially paralyzed from head to toe on my right side.

I was in trouble, and I knew it. I wanted to call for help but I didn't know how to use the phone, or even if I did, who I would call. So, I laid on my couch and waited for someone to show up. I reasoned somebody must know me and eventually they would come knocking on my door. They did, and I was admitted to the hospital where they ran many, many tests over the next week.

I was diagnosed with encephalitis. The doctors told me I had been bitten by a mosquito and was lucky to be alive. Of the 12 cases in Florida that year, half of the victims had died.

I now had no feeling in my right arm or leg; my mouth drooped, causing me to slur my words; and I walked with a pronounced limp. In addition, I had no short term memory. Whatever was said to me – or whatever I said – was forgotten within twenty seconds. As a result, I would say the same thing over and over again.

Every item in my memory bank was gone – except for one. I remembered I was a Christian. I couldn't have quoted bible verses or theological theories, but I knew Jesus loved me. To this day, I don't believe that was by chance – a fortunate accident of nature. I believe God said, "You can take everything else, but you can't take Me."

Then, one night as I was laying in my hospital bed, God spoke to me.

He said, "Ask me and I will do it."

Now that doesn't sound very God-like, does it? However, I believe He knew I only could understand small words and simple thoughts.

I asked God to heal me and I felt a peace come over me. I knew that He would.

The next day two doctors came in. "Mr. Creed, we have some good and bad news for you," he paused. "The good news is you won't get any worse. The bad news is you won't get much better. Now, you may find small things improve: You may learn how to count or even add and subtract; or perhaps, the names of your children. However, beyond small improvements, the way you are now is the way things are going to be in the future. You can waste your time wishing things were now as they used to be, and make yourself miserable; or, you can accept your new life and find reasons for happiness."

I didn't believe him. I was sure God had promised He would heal me. So, over their objection, I signed out of the hospital and went home.

Fortunately, my oldest daughter moved back home to help me. Without her, I would have been in real trouble. I couldn't remember anything. She would open the refrigerator and find my shoes and underwear neatly stacked or my shaving equipment in the dining room drawers. If I wanted anything, it would entail a full scale search of every room and every drawer.

I would pray nightly that God would honor His promise. "When, Lord, when?" I would shout. Yet, the next day was the same, and the next, and the next.

After many months of trying to get God to do things my way, I gave up. I'd wanted Jesus and me to be partners in this healing. But, if God was going to heal me, He would have to do it because I was pooped out! That's exactly what God was waiting for me to do: Give up, and cast my concerns at His feet. Finally, I was allowing God to be God, and myself to be, not his partner, but his servant.

Weeks went by, then months. To help me through this time, I believe God sent a song. I hadn't been listening to music or watching TV because I couldn't understand the words. They sounded like gibberish to me. However, when I heard this song, "I Need To Be Still," I understood the words and they spoke to my soul. It gave me the message to wait upon God. It told me it was time to let go and let God take over. I would play that song over and over again – every day, all day.

Still, I would pray, shout, and plead as the days passed, then months, and a new year came.

Those around me were very patient. I had a business to run. Obviously, I could not do that. So, my employees stepped up and took

20

over many responsibilities. While I sat in my office and stared at the ceiling or wandered around smiling at everyone, my daughter took over the office responsibilities while my managers took on added responsibilities to keep things functioning. My clients found that anything they said to me was forgotten the moment I left their office. But, rather than fire me, they chose to stick with me. They would write their needs on an eight by ten sheet of paper and safety-pin it to my shirt. When I arrived back at the office, my office manager would take the sheet and do whatever needed to be done.

I recall, one day, about a year after I was struck, I needed a hammer to hang a picture. I went into the garage and retrieved it. I was halfway back, when I froze. I gasped for breath as I felt chills go through me. I stared at the hammer while realizing I had remembered.

I remembered! I remembered! I didn't look in the refrigerator, or dishwasher, or under the bed, I simply went to the toolbox and got the hammer. Just like a REAL PERSON! I began dancing around and shouting with joy.

I knew that my healing had begun. It was as if God had finally said, "Enough!"

Now, it didn't occur in one day, or a week, a month or even a year; however, it did begin. Slowly, as the years have passed, I've gotten better and better, but God's not finished yet. I still have trouble with my memory and a lot of trouble with numbers – but as I said, God's not finished yet. So, nearly every day of those thirty years, I've played, hummed or sung the song, "I Need To Be Still."

It's taken many years – and I'm still not 100% – but God has restored me to become a better man than I was before. I came from being unable to read or write to having now written three books. I had trouble speaking the English language, yet since, I have recorded songs in Nashville, which have praised His name over the airways from coast to coast. God promised it, and God did it. I thank Jesus every day for his faithfulness and mercy.

So, what has this experience taught me? I learned God has His unerring reasons of why and when. I need to trust in His will and timing, and believe He knows what is best for me, and how to achieve it in my life.

SUNSHINE CHAIR CIRCLE
By Elaine Dugas Shea

Honky-tonk piano man
Sings Gospel like I've
Never heard. A man
Without hips or legs
Sways side to side in
His wheel chair -- coming
From a deep socket of joy
Miss Sarie pokes her head
In the door checking things out

The human face shines on, muscles and
Skin work together traveling
Back in time, everyone young again.
Arms lift in praise feeling the swing
A rough path doesn't matter
The wrist-bands shake-dance, *not* Carolina
Shag, but body is surely not
The only barometer.

THE BROKEN EARRING
By Caroline Misner

Everybody wanted to buy a diamond. It was early December, the onset of the Christmas rush, and business in the jewelry shop was brisk. There were five of us altogether, including my manager, Alexandra, and me. We struggled all afternoon to keep pace with the throngs of shoppers that wandered into the store. High ticket items were selling well, much to the delight of the staff since we earned a small commission on each sale we made. By mid afternoon, the store was stuffy and almost unbearably hot beneath the halogen lights that lit up the cases. The whole mall was a maelstrom of gaudy red and green adornments drooping in the windows; garbled voices muffled the Christmas music that blasted from the speakers.

I had just finished serving a customer and was enjoying a brief lull when the woman hobbled up to me. She had been there a while, though few of us had noticed her and no one had bothered to serve her.

"Hi." Her voice was timid and little more than a breathy whisper.

She leaned against the handlebars of her walker. Her legs were stubby and bent at odd angles, making it difficult for her to walk. She wore heavy glasses with lenses so thick they made her eyes look watery. A bright pink scar from a recent tracheotomy marred the base of her throat, yellow and soft as butter. She carried herself like someone recovering from some terrible ravishing illness.

"Hi," I responded. I was reluctant to serve her. It was obvious she had little money. Her coat was several sizes too big and ragged at the hem. She wore baggy jeans and a faded sweatshirt stained by a recent meal. "May I help you?"

"I need earrings." The woman's fingers trembled as she pointed at her ear where a tiny pinpoint puckered the lobe. "Before my holes grow in."

"Certainly," I replied and gathered my keys to open the case of diamond studs.

"What can I get for ten dollars?" she asked. She pulled a wrinkled bill from her coat pocket and placed it on the counter. "It's all I have."

Ten dollars would buy nothing in the shop. Simple gold loops started at twenty dollars and went up into the hundreds from there. She stared up at me with such hope and anticipation, I couldn't tell her. I was about to push the money back when I thought of something.

There are tiny loop earrings called sleepers, where a thin rod fits into the hollow tube on the other side and makes it virtually impossible for the earring to fall out. They are popular choices for small children since they are secure and comfortable. And they retail for ten dollars.

The woman smiled and a shade of color softened her sallow cheeks when I showed them to her.

"Can you put them in for me?" she asked.

She gripped my elbow with one hand and her walker with the other as I guided her to the massive brown leather chair we used to pierce our patron's ears. Her legs wobbled beneath her and she sighed deeply when she sank into the leather seat.

"Are they hard to put in?" she asked when she noticed the trouble I was having in getting the loop through the hole. She hadn't worn any earrings in months and a membrane had formed over the holes; I was afraid I'd have to pierce her ears all over again and I knew she couldn't afford that.

"A little," I admitted. "But once they're in, they don't fall out."

"Can a home care worker get them in?"

"Easily," I smiled.

I had managed to break the layer of skin over the hole in her right ear and loop the earring through. I moved on to the left. The hole in that ear had grown in more than the first. I almost managed to insert the earring when the thin gold band snapped in two.

"Oh, no!" I was horrified. I'd broken the only piece of jewelry this poor woman could afford.

"What's the matter?" she asked.

"I'll be right back." I rushed behind the counter to show Alexandra. Concern creased her pretty features when she saw how visibly upset I was.

"I accidentally broke it," I said, "and she can't afford another. What do I do?"

Alexandra assured me it would be all right. We found another pair similar in price to the broken earring and with her permission I was able to give them to the woman without charging her for a second pair.

In a few minutes I managed to pull the earring through her lobe and snap it into place. I held up a mirror so she could admire herself in her new earrings.

"Do I look pretty?" she asked.

"Yes," I replied in all sincerity. "You look beautiful."

I helped the women back to her feet. She gripped the handle of her walker and shuffled out of the store.

"Thank you so much," she said on her way out and gave my hand a weak squeeze. "I still want to look good even though I'm ill. You've been very helpful."

It had taken me over half an hour to assist that poor woman. During that time, several pieces of expensive diamond jewelry had been sold by the other saleswomen. They would receive a hefty bonus in their next paychecks. But I didn't care. What that poor woman had given me was far more valuable than any bauble in the store.

Several months later, I related this story to a friend during a party.

"You know," I said. "I really believe that I was looking at God when I saw that woman."

"No," my friend replied and shook his head. "You weren't looking at God. God was looking at you."

SUNSHINE
By Sheryl L Nelms

twenty-two years old
black
and beautiful

face always smiling

sparkling
brown eyes say
he's in there
with soul

even though
the mouth
can't talk
and the diapered
body is nothing
but a breathing skeleton
curled tight

in a frozen fetal twist

the nurses
call him

Sunshine

FAITH, HOPE AND A PARKING LOT MIRACLE
Francine L. Billingslea

We sat and watched the big peach drop in Atlanta, Georgia and counted with millions of people all over the world, 5...4...3...2...1...then screamed out "Happy New Year!" My mother, my fiancé and I did a group hug, then fell to our knees and said prayers asking for health, divine intervention and protection for ourselves and loved ones throughout the year. As we got to our feet, my mother smiled and said, "I believe this is going to be a very special and a very good year." She blew us a kiss, and then went to bed. My fiancé turned to me and said, "I feel the same way." I agreed.

I had made several doctors' appointments for a complete physical, and, other than having a little arthritis, I received good reports from all of them -- now just the mammogram was left and I would be done for the year.

I sat in the cold dark dressing room rubbing my left arm and thought I should have taken something for the pain as I patiently waited for the slow-moving technician. Finally she called me in, and immediately began positioning my right side, tightening the plate, she said, "Okay hold." She ran in the back, and then yelled out, "Okay, you can breathe!" I turned so she could position my left side, as she pulled, stretched and yanked, I told her about the arthritis on that side. As she tightened the plate, pain began to dance up and down my arm, across my chest and shoulder and made my knees buckle. "This will only take a minute," she said before yelling out the familiar instructions. "Okay, as soon as the doctor takes a look at the films, you can get dressed." She hurried out of the room. When she returned, she said, "We need to do the left side again." After the second time, I was then escorted down the hall to have a sonogram done. After a question and answer session with the doctor, he told me to come back on Monday for a biopsy. Needless to say, my weekend was filled with prayer, apprehensions, pain and hoping for the best.

Wednesday morning I received the totally unforeseen diagnosis, I had breast cancer. A week later I was recuperating from the surgery, and two weeks after that, I was sitting in my oncologist's office completely unaware of the battle that was about to begin. The first four rounds of chemotherapy were ruthless, not only did I lose my hair, but I constantly suffered from nausea, fatigue, dehydration, anemia and loss of appetite. My mother and my fiancé frequently rushed me back and forth to the doctors and the hospital. My next four rounds of chemo were lighter doses, and although I still got sick, I gratefully tolerated them a lot better than the first four.

Having been raised to believe in the power of faith and prayer, I prayed constantly. I fought physically and spiritually and neither one was an easy battle. On my worst days, I confessed I was healed. When I did not feel like praying, I prayed anyway. And when my faith got weak, I looked up promises in the Bible and found healing testimonies. I read them over and over to keep hope alive in my heart. In addition, I went to church as often as possible, and I became more forgiving and made sure my soul was right with God, which was cleansing and healing within itself.

One day when I had a doctor's appointment, I decided to go by myself. I was tired of being smothered and I wanted to give my supporters a break; so against their wishes, I drove to the medical center alone. While driving, I prayed and sang praise songs. I had one more round of chemo, then six weeks of radiation and I'd be done. It was a long hard journey, but I was finally reaching the other side. My appetite was back, I had picked up a few pounds and I had a few strands of hair – I couldn't have been happier.

A block from my destination, I began to feel strange and light-headed. I pulled over and sat a minute, it subsided and I continued. By the time I reached the parking lot, the feeling had returned, my head and body ached and I felt exceptionally weak. I opened the door of my SUV and when I went to step out, everything went black. When I opened my eyes, I was lying on the ground; a young man was kneeling besides me holding my hand and telling me that I was going to be alright. An older woman seemed frantic as she was screaming something. I kept going in and out of consciousness as I was put onto a stretcher and rushed inside the hospital. Later that night, I came around long enough to notice I was hooked up to several IV's and see my mother and fiancé's worried faces. Too weak and groggy to say anything, I fell back asleep.

Several days passed before I found out that I had an infection that had gotten into my blood stream. This was very serious, but all through my battles I never gave up on faith, hope and prayer.

One day a woman came in to see me. She introduced herself and began to explain that she had come out of the medical building and gotten into her car. As she started it up and put it into reverse, two men abruptly stopped her. One stood at the back of her car so she couldn't back up and the other was telling her that a woman had passed out and was lying by the back wheel on her passenger side. She began to cry as she repeated herself over and over that she didn't see me. If it weren't for those two young men, she would have backed up and rolled over me not once, but twice with the front and back wheels.

I shuddered and sat straight up in the bed as she continued her story. She said she jumped out of her car, came around to the passenger side, and there I was, lying on an angle with my face almost touching her back wheel. She said she got so nervous; all she could do was cry and scream for help. When I asked her about the young men, she said one of them was kneeling beside me holding my hand, while the other one started picking up my wallet and other objects that had fallen out of my purse. She then said people started coming from everywhere. Several nurses and a doctor came out and placed me on a stretcher and rushed me inside.

While she was telling a nurse what happened, she turned around to thank the young men, but they were gone. When she asked several on-lookers where the two young men went, they looked puzzled and asked, "What men?"

I told her that I vaguely remember a man holding my hand and talking to me. She quickly nodded her head up and down in a yes fashion and tearfully exclaimed, "Honey, I might be old, but I know I'm not crazy! Those men saved both of our lives. As you can see, I'm an elderly woman, if I had run over you..." She stopped, and now seemed satisfied that her sanity was verified.

There was a long pause before she mentioned that she and her husband came to see me later that evening, but I was sleeping. She told my mother and my fiancé what had happened; they told her they knew, obviously the same nurse had spoken to them.

Before she left, she hugged me and said, "Honey, something bad happened in my life and I stopped praying and going to church years ago, but I'm definitely going to start again; I never really believed in angels before, but I do now. I'm so grateful they were in the parking lot that day!"

I smiled and said, "I am too!" As she walked out of my room, I undoubtedly knew that it was a life changing experience for her. I also knew those men or angels were sent from above because of my faith.

My mother was right, that year did turn out to be a very good and a very special year; our prayers for health, divine intervention and protection were surely answered. Our faith was overwhelmingly strengthened, and, through faith, hope and prayers my life was spared twice: the first time from breast cancer, and the second time, miraculously from a tragic accident. And because of this, a lost sheep was also brought back into the pasture.

THOUGHTS OF YOU
By Margie Scott

You sent me a cooling breeze this morning
With soft clouds in the sky
Song birds in the distance
You hear my quiet sigh
My pain softens and begins to ease
As thoughts of You flood my heart and soul
Oh how glorious it will be
Your face to behold
The pangs of this world gone and forgotten
Peace and love and praising You
Oh, what a day that will be.

GLIMMER OF HOPE
By Lynn C. Johnston

Shattered lives and shattered hearts
Shattered worlds torn apart
Tattered clothes and tattered dreams
Life blown asunder, so it seems

From the dark of night, all is lost
Devastation too high to count the cost
Yet amidst all the misery that abounds
A glimmer of hope can somehow be found

In an open heart and an outstretched hand
A compassionate smile helps us understand
We're not alone in our desperate plight
Someone can help us win our fight

With a little faith and a little hope
We'll find some peace and a way to cope
Thanks in part to someone who cared
Who was willing to give and willing to share

WAITING FOR OUR MIRACLE
By Perry P. Perkins

When I was a boy, my mother had a small plaque that hung in the kitchen of our tiny apartment.

It read, *"Even miracles take a little time"*

My wife and I had planned on being the typical American couple. We'd get married, work for a couple of years (*to earn some stability and get to know one another*) and then start our family. We had seen our friends follow this same agenda and it seemed simple enough.

We learned it was not always so simple...

Years of self-doubt, frustration, and bittersweet smiles as we held the newborn babies of our closest friends, all the while agonizing over the empty place in our own home and hearts, the frustration of not being able to give each other the baby we wanted so badly, while longing to be the parents that we KNEW God had made us to be.

Finally, after a decade of trying and reaching the ripe-old age of thirty-eight, we realized that having a baby just wasn't going to happen the "old-fashioned way."

So, we sought help.

Only to find that "help" is expensive...help is *very* expensive.

The process of IVF (in-vitro fertilization) and a subsequent pregnancy and birth would cost tens of thousands of dollars. We had three hundred dollars in the bank.

It was a long night at the dinner table. There was anger and there were tears. How could God put such a burning desire, such a lifelong goal to be parents in our hearts, and then make it impossible to achieve?

We didn't have tens of thousands of dollars...we didn't have *one* thousand dollars...but we did have our house.

Years of scrimping and saving, driving clunker cars and brown-bagging lunches had allowed us to pay off our school debts and save just enough for a down payment on a beautiful little three-bedroom, two-bath house on the outskirts of town.

In short, we had waited, and worked hard, for our miracle.

Vickie and I both worked full time, living in tiny apartments in bad neighborhoods to save money, crunching numbers until they squeaked and jumping though every hoop imaginable for ten years to buy that house. It wasn't much, but it was *ours*. For a kid who'd never lived anywhere but apartment complexes, it was *everything*: a place to have friends over, to plant our own flowers, and to paint the walls whatever shade of purple we pleased…a place of our own. It had been like a dream come true when, three years before, we'd signed papers and moved in, and now it was being made clear to us…

We could have our baby…if we gave up our home.

The market was ripe, and our agent assured us that we could get our asking price, which would leave us just enough to pay off our loan, our few remaining debts, and complete the IVF process one time.

We talked. We argued. We cried.

Finally, we prayed.

That's when we realized that everything we had scrimped and saved and sacrificed for had been leading to *this* moment. We weren't being forced out of our home, we were being given an *opportunity* to have the child we'd always wanted… and all we had to trade for our miracle baby was this block of brick and stone.

People all over the world suffered through childless lives, and we had been given a blank check. A check with three bedrooms, two baths, and a garage… all we had to do was sign it.

And we did.

More sacrifices were made, possessions were sold, and more tears were shed when we stood in the living room of yet another tiny two-bedroom apartment. Then the innumerable trips to the doctor, the embarrassing medical tests, the *extremely* candid conversations with nurses, and the seemingly-unending *"are we"* or *"aren't we"* months of limbo, hope and heart-break.

During the IVF appointment, only four viable eggs were found. On the morning of implantation, only one had survived. Our doctor put it to us straight, the odds were long against us, but, as he put it, "We're here anyway, if you want to give it a try."

We knew we couldn't afford another treatment. We knew we needed a miracle. So, we prayed and cried, and said yes. Then, once again, we waited.

It's been three years since we sold our dream house, and our daughter Grace just turned one. Nothing about her addition to our family was easy, not her conception, her birth, or her first weeks at home. But she has brought light to our lives that no windows could, and colors to our world that no flowers can ever match...she is truly our miracle baby.

Then baby Grace smiles, laughs and hugs our necks, and we know that our miracle was worth the wait.

RENEWAL
By Marguerite Guzmán Bouvard

After months of raw pain and no sleep,
when each day rises above me
like a precipitous mountain,
suddenly my spirit returns
like new grass, spreading
its cloak on the bruised earth,
speaking the language
of winds. Again and again
You bring me back
to the simplicity and grace
of the soul's new shoots.

FLIGHT SCHOOL
By Katherine K. Walker

How do I capture forever
That calls to my deepest pain?
How do I reach heaven's portals
When I can't seem to fly in the rain?
So I thought....
I must consult with the Savior
'bout this vacant place in me
And ask if He'd be willing
To share from His love soaked tree
So I fell on my knees in an instant.....and said
Oh Lord, I'm just a sinner
Who's longing for to sing
Please teach me how to fly away
With a pair of your gifted wings
Then His love came down and touched me
Into my deepest part
And there He placed a silver pair
Of wings on my still beating heart
A fire of light was kindled
By the spirit on that special night
And some sweet day I'll fly away home
With the wings He prepared for my flight

THE HOLY DIRT OF CHIMAYO
By Joanne Seltzer

A Jew
I scooped some up
asked the tour guide
"Do you have to believe?"

He didn't know
Half of our group
said yes
half said no

Taken home to a sick friend
who believes in Christ
and witchcraft too

the grit gave her
belly cramps
purgation
and a cure

IT IS WELL WITH MY SOUL
By Linda Zenone

Lately, for some reason, I have really been having a hard time. It's almost like a dark cloud has decided to park itself right over top of my head. It all started last Friday. The day actually started out very well. I went over to spend time with my client, Mae, and brought her some rigatoni with home-made meat sauce. She was so thrilled. It had been a long time since she had anything much besides Meals-on-Wheels! Don't get me wrong, Meals-on-Wheels provides some pretty good meals, but like Mae said, "It's just not like home-cooking!" When I left her that day I was feeling pretty happy because she seemed to be coming out of her shell a little more.

I got out to the parking lot and then it hit... that dark cloud.

I locked myself out of my car while it was running... and it was almost out of gas. And it was one of the hottest, most humid days we had had in awhile. I was in a panic. I had no idea what to do. My purse and cell phone and everything were all locked up in the car. And of course, so was the extra key I have just in case something like this ever happens. Lot of good it was doing me now.

I ran back up to Mae's to see if she had a coat hanger. I wasn't really sure what I was going to *do* with it, but I've seen a lot of people use coat hangers when they were locked out of their cars. It was worth a try. She gave me the hanger and told me to please let her know if it worked. She seemed very concerned and I assured her I would.

Back down I went to try to see what kind of magic I could perform with the wire hanger. I got it as straight as I could, poked it in-between the door, and jammed it down inside the car but wasn't real sure how that was going to be any help. It wasn't strong enough to push down the button that unlocks the doors, even if I *could* get it anywhere near it. Already I was dripping with sweat and feeling light-headed from the heat.

I think I was about ready to faint from heat exhaustion when a man pulled up across from where I was parked. He was obviously coming home from work; I could tell by the long-sleeved dress shirt he had on and by the briefcase he was carrying. He looked tired and was probably thrilled to be home and couldn't wait to get inside to the air-conditioning, sit down and put his feet up. But I was desperate at that point and hollered over to him, "Mister! Can you pleeease help me!" I know it sounded like a whine because it *was* one. He looked at me kind of startled, I guess to see a grown woman standing there looking like she was ready to cry any minute (which, in fact, I was.) I could tell the last thing he wanted to do was to postpone getting inside his cozy home after a long day at work, but he very gallantly came over to see what he could do to help me.

He poked and prodded a little with the hanger and then informed me that it just wasn't strong enough to do anything (I could've told him that!); I would probably have to call a locksmith. That's the last thing I wanted to do... number one because of the cost, and number two because I was sure my car would run out of gas by the time they got there. But, what choice did I have? I reluctantly agreed to allow him to call one for me. I followed him up *three* flights of stairs to his apartment, (it *had* to be on the very top floor didn't it?) and waited outside while he called. He ended up calling three or four to find the cheapest one. As I recovered from that terrible climb, which in the intense heat was comparable to climbing Mt. Everest, I realized this man, this *stranger*, really was going out of his way to help me. Maybe he was an angel in disguise or something... I think I was becoming delirious from the heat.

He finally found someone who would do it for $30 but it might be as long as a half hour before he could get there. I had to agree to it. I thanked the man profusely for his help and hurried down to my car to try again to perform some kind of magic with that hanger before the locksmith got there. If I could get it before he got there I could save myself $30 and hopefully not run out of gas! I got the bright idea to bend the end of the hanger into a hook so I could try to catch it on the door handle and yank it open. I managed to hook the handle quite a few frustrating times but it just wasn't strong enough. It bent back every time! I was dripping with sweat and so intent on what I was doing I didn't even notice a van had pulled up beside my car. I looked up through the wet strands of my hair to see a young man sitting in the driver seat of the car watching me with an amused expression on his face.

I was about to plead with him for help, like I did that other poor man, when it dawned on me that it was the locksmith. Instead of being upset that he found my predicament amusing and realizing how I must look, I started to laugh and sighed with relief as he used some flat tool and quickly had the door open in a few seconds.

Okay, now I could go home! I got into the car and immediately heard "It Is Well with My Soul" coming from my car radio. At first I thought how inappropriate that song was at a time like this. Things certainly *weren't* well with my soul at the moment. The song continued and I was surprised at how comforting the words actually were and how calming it was to listen to. I thought about how Paul says to be content no matter what state you are in.

As I drove I began to think about Mae. She's 88 years old and lives all alone and has stopped caring about so much. When I first started going over there she hardly spoke. No matter what I suggested we do she agreed, only because she just didn't care one way or another. Today she had actually smiled when I brought her a big plate of rigatoni and she thanked me over and over again for making it for her. She had even laughed and joked a couple times after that. And when I returned to her apartment to borrow the hanger she was so genuinely concerned and made me promise to call her when I got home to let her know everything was fine. That was more emotion and signs of life than I had seen in her since I started going over two weeks ago.

When I got home I called her and told her everything that had happened...about the nice man who helped me and about having to finally call a locksmith. She told me she had almost come out of her apartment to walk down and see if I was alright. Tears welled up in my eyes at the thought of this old lady struggling with her walker to actually leave her apartment for *me*. The neighbors had told me that Mae had stopped coming out of her apartment and had pretty much stopped doing anything a couple years ago. "All she does is sit in that chair and stare," one concerned neighbor had told me. This couldn't be the same lady who was now chatting on the phone with me, laughing with me about how funny I must've looked struggling with that hanger! It seems like my dark cloud had somehow brought a little sun into Mae's life. Or maybe it was the rigatoni.

That Friday began a series of mishaps: a weekend with no electricity in our house; the hot water heater burning out so we had no hot water; never receiving my paychecks for the past two weeks, and my back that's been really hurting lately.

But, black cloud or not... it *is* well with my soul.

NOTHING DIES HERE
By Rick Kempa

The hospital yardboy's
orders are to mow,
prune, rake, bag,
but not to weed.
A weed is what
you call something
that you cannot name
and there are none here
where we retire

Each alone
in the fragile shade
of afternoons
that have no past,
no future, to close
our eyes, because
they have looked too long
on suffering,
and not to dream.

It is not a lawn,
a cultured thing
he must keep up, but
a green interfuse
of clover, violet,
dandelion, grasses,
a root network
that remains intact
after his passage.

At night, water
from a secret source,
like hope that persists
without good cause,
covers leaflets,
blades, blooms
so that, weeping,
they rejoice,
Nothing dies here!

MATINS
By Gwendolyn Carr

You can't fool me.

The earnestness within your eyes
belies that fearful well
where demons from a darkened past
dwell between what was and is,
ready to cast their images
on all that's new and bright.

And if what you are telling me
in those beseeching eyes
is anything like hope,
we shall go on. Darkness
cannot crush the light
that's bending toward the dawn.

THE JANITOR
By Naty Smith

Jason had not set foot inside a church since he was a small child. He had never felt any need or strong desire to go to service or even pray for that matter. Churches were boring places where people shout and scream for apparently no reason at all and he didn't think that was necessary to let God "hear" you.

Today he felt defeated and out of hope as he walked by the doors of the church. He walked up to the doors expecting them to be locked as most churches were nowadays when there was no service going on, but surprisingly they were open. He sat on the front pew and put his head in his hands. He needed some time to think. He managed a successful business, he was with the woman he loved, had two beautiful children and he still had not achieved happiness.

He reviewed the later years of his life. A noise from the back of the church startled him out of his sobs. From the back of the church emerged a man. He looked to be in his 60's. His hair was gray and his back was slightly hunched over the rolling bucket and mop he was dragging alongside him. Jason tried to pull it together once he heard the old man approaching, but he just couldn't stop the flow once it started. The older man heard the sobs and sat down next to him on the pew.

"Are you okay young man?" asked the older man placing his hand on the younger man's shoulder.

Jason composed himself and looked up. "Yes sir, thank you, just having a bad day."

"Life is full of those, son. I can get someone out here to talk to you."

"No thank you. I don't belong to this church....well, I don't belong in church anyway."

"Why would you say that?"

"I have not been in a temple since I was ten years old. I'm sorry sir, I don't even know you and here I am burdening you with my issues. I just… I think I lost my way somehow."

"Nah you didn't, here you are, aren't you?"

"I just felt desperate today. At lunch, I called my wife and she sounded sad, so I took a walk and it led me here," the man paused. "It breaks my heart that she's so sad. When I met her, she was vibrant, happy. Now that we finally are where we dreamt to be, she is sad all the time. I've been working really hard. I am a successful businessman and have made a name for myself in this community. I take care of my family and I have a big house in the suburbs. My children go to private schools. I've built this life for them, but it still doesn't seem to be enough. I don't know what to do. My wife is everything to me. My children…They are everything to me."

The older man sighed, "Well, seems like you've done a lot by yourself too. It must be very hard to do all that by yourself."

"Yes, I've worked very hard for everything I have and I did it all for them – and now it feels like I did it for nothing." Looking at his watch, "Hey, I'm sorry to take up your time with my stuff. My name is Jason by the way."

"Well, Jason, it's been a pleasure. Like I said before, if you're interested in talking to someone, just come over. There's always someone waiting to hear from you. Consider coming to service. It might do you good."

"Nah," he chuckled. "Like I said, I'm not into the church thing."

Jason left, the words of the old man vibrating in his head. He made it home late that evening. His wife was in bed like most days. He laid next to her and told her about his encounter in church. He repeated to her the words that the old man had said to him.

"You know Jason, as much as I love you, there has been this distance growing between us. Sometimes it feels like you are this great god, some kind of titan that can take on the world all by yourself. It makes me realize how little I'm actually needed."

Jason sat up straight to look at his wife. This conversation was totally different from the ones they'd had before; this felt strange. His wife had been depressed for a long time but he didn't know the reason. The truth is he had never asked. Jason immediately tried to defend himself, "But I've done all this for you."

"No Jason, you did it for you. You did it to make yourself look good in front of everyone. I never see you, the kids are in bed when you leave in the morning and tucked in by the time you get home at night. They don't know you, and frankly, neither do I." Then she turned and went to sleep.

The next day on his lunch break he walked back over to the church. It was only a couple blocks from his job, surprising he had never seen it before yesterday. Once again the church was empty save for the old man.

"Hey Jason, I wasn't expecting you back so soon."

"I was hoping you were here because... I need to talk to you. I told my wife about our talk yesterday and for the first time she actually talked to me about how she feels. She said I am selfish and that everything I have done I have done for me. I'm not selfish, I didn't do this for me, I did it for them...well, and yes, I did it for me, but not solely. I wanted the best for my family and myself and now I have nothing."

"Son, only you know in your heart why you did the things you did. Now don't answer this, but ask yourself – was it for love or greed? Did you ever ask yourself if what you did was your purpose in life or did you pursue something because it was going to make you more money and more successful?" The old man spoke evenly.

He looked at the old man with sadness in his eyes. He felt a heavy weight in his heart. "Oh my God, what have I done?" Jason covered his face with his hands. "All these years, I thought I was doing this for them – but it's all been about me. I sacrificed my family for money and success. I feel so empty. I don't want this anymore." He looked at the man and pleadingly said, "Is it too late now? How do I find out what my purpose is? Tell me how to fix this?"

The man looked tenderly into his eyes, and placed his hand over his shoulder "Just come home." With those words, the man got up, grabbed his mop and rolled his bucket of water to the back of the church.

Jason went back home. He got there before any of the family arrived home. When his wife and kids came in they were surprised to see him home so early. He grabbed his kids up in his arms and hugged them. He grabbed his wife and kissed her deeply. He told her that he wanted to attend church service that following Sunday. She was surprised, but she agreed.

Sunday morning, Jason, his wife and kids were early in service. He felt like a fish out of water. He found himself fascinated by the prayers and awed by the choir's beautiful sound. The words of the pastor enraptured him and took him on a journey he had never even knew he wanted to go on. When the pastor asked if there were any new visitors, he raised his hand slowly.

At the end of service, the pastor went to welcome them personally. "I'm Pastor Gene Walsh. Welcome to our church, we are glad to have you with us. Is your family new to the area?"

"No, I have an office nearby. Your janitor and I have talked a couple of times this week. So I decided to try out your service. We are

44

new to the whole church thing, and we will definitely be back." His family nodded enthusiastically.

"Oh, that's wonderful. So you have met Maria? She's a great woman!" said Pastor Walsh enthusiastically

"Maria?" Jason was confused

"Yes, our janitor. Maria does the cleaning in our church."

"No, I met the old man. You know I never asked him his name, how rude of me..."

"Well Jason, I'm not sure who that could be, there is no older gentleman who helps clean the church. Well regardless, I am glad you decided to come today."

"I am too, Pastor."

Jason shook the Pastor's hand. He embraced his wife and started the walk to the car. He looked back and called out to Pastor Walsh. "Pastor, it's good to be home."

WHISPERS, TEARS, PRAYERS AND HOPE
By Ed Roberts

A school bell rings.
Children gather for their daily dose of hope.
They know that simply by being there
They put their lives in danger.
Still they sit,
Listen carefully to each lesson,
And train themselves
To be the future of their people
Because they know
How many lives were sacrificed
How much blood was spilled
To give them this opportunity.

A frail man stands in line
Just like he did yesterday.
He will wait hours
Simply to receive a small bag of rice
And a few precious bottles of water.
He will take these blessed gifts
Home to his family
And like yesterday
Save very little for himself.
Still he smiles
Because he knows

They will all survive
Another day.

A woman slowly packs her clothes
Into the small suitcase upon her bed.

She gathers her two children
And silently slips out the door
Trying her best
Not to make a sound
Afraid she will wake him.
The three end up in a strange new place
Filled with others
That are fleeing the same conditions.
She knows the next few months will be tough
But now deep down
She knows at least now they stand a chance.

I sit here at my computer
With tears running down my face
And try to capture just a few words.
Words that might serve as a simple reminder
Of the many blessings we all have in our lives.
Words left here to remind us
That there still is so much for us to give.
The most important of which
Is hope.

These are words that flow so freely.
Each like a single teardrop
That falls upon this keyboard.
Each one of them a whisper.
Each one
A simple prayer.

THE CALMING STORM
By Constance Gilbert

The children were grumbling, as they washed their hands for supper. It had been a day of bickering kids, frantic phone calls, and everything going wrong. My stress level had maxed out hours ago. *A good nutritious dinner would do us all some good,* I thought and tried to keep smiling.

Balancing a platter on one hand and trying to carry two bowls in the other, I turned from the stove to hear, "I don't like pork chops..."

"Take us out to McDonalds!"

"I'm not eating that!"

"I wanna go to A&W for hotdogs and beer."

"No, to McDonalds!"

I'd had it! Nearly dropping the platter, I put the food down and ran out of the kitchen, through the living room, and out the front door. My emotions were out of control, and I knew I'd lash out instead of dealing with the children appropriately. So I ended up facing a huge, smelly dumpster crying my heart out – a miserable, over-whelmed single-mother. That is, until I decided, *I'm leaving!*

I was the strong one in the family, the organizer and planner, the peace-keeper. I had never acted rashly and spontaneously. Yet, there I was running back indoors. I grabbed my keys and yelled to the eldest, "You're in charge."

Driving out of town, with rivers of tears re-emerging and splashing over the steering wheel into my lap, I saw nothing except the road, my escape path. How long or how far I went, I don't remember, but the anger began to dissipate. Then when I saw a state forest/park sign, I hit the brakes and turned right without thinking of other cars and drivers.

Winding down the one lane entrance to the park, I tried to calmly pull myself together. At the gated entrance, I pulled up feeling quite embarrassed – no purse, no money. I told the gatekeeper I'd just make a u-turn and leave. He just nodded, but then said, "It's almost closing time; go on in for a few minutes."

Actually, there were several more hours of daylight left. The park officially closed at dusk; we'd watched the sunset over that lake many times before. Yet, I didn't think of that as I parked the car.

Normally, I loved the sound of the waves, the feel of the warm sand, and the colors of the water melding into the blue sky. However, my tears began anew as I saw all the families laughing and playing together on the beach; and heard shouts of "Look at me, Mom!" from the water.

How dare they be so happy, when I'm so miserable!

As I headed toward the far end of the swimming area, giant raindrops plopped on the sand in front of me... then on my head and shoulders. *That's more like it. I can cry and no one will know.* So I settled down on the sand, pulling a tissue from my pocket as thunder began to rumble. Soon lightning flashed on the far-side of the lake. Parents called for their children to get out of the water, as they grabbed beach towels, sand toys, water bottles and all the stuff for a day at the beach. Gathering their families, like mother hens, they raced for their cars as the rain came down faster than they could run.

The laughter of children was replaced by good-byes to friends new and old. Then the sound of tires rolling over the gravel, a few honks and they were gone.

The storm crossed the lake toward me. *I don't even know how to run away right,* I moaned, but I stayed... crying... alone.

As the temperature dropped, the only warm spot was the sand under me. Soon it too would be as water-logged as I was, but still I stayed.

Deep in my own thoughts, I never heard the old man from the booth approach. I just looked up and there he was. Even with an old, well-worn raincoat and hat on, he was wet and bedraggled, but his eyes... his eyes were filled with compassion as his hand reached out to help me up. Shivering, but not afraid, I took his hand and he led me to a swing hanging in a small arbor. "It's drier here. Just sit a while longer," he said.

After a short while he added, "Things aren't always as they seem, you know." And we watched the storm traveling across the water.

The rhythm of the raindrops and the gentle swaying of the swing soothed my jumbled emotions. My heartbeat slowed as a sense of calm surrounded me. The tears still flowed, unashamedly; yet, now they were cleansing. The sweet smell of the flowers dripping overhead drifted into my consciousness. Slowly, I noticed a unique silence in the midst of the storm – something more than us just not speaking. The overwhelming burdens of my life seemed to shrink as the storm began to pass.

He softly, almost in a whisper, told me, "It's time to go home to your boys."

I nodded. *Yes, I could go home now.*

I noticed the soggy tissues in my hand and I grinned, just a little, at the thought of how I must look. I turned to thank him for his kindness, but he was already gone. Thunder still rumbled in the distance as I raced to my car.

My old blue Toyota was the only vehicle left in the parking lot. How could he have left so quickly? He was an old man, after all, and I was right behind him, wasn't I? From my car I scanned the beach for him. Nothing. I searched the paths leading into the trees. No one. He must have made it to the booth at the gate.

When I pulled up to the tollbooth window, I saw the sign:

Due to budget cuts,
we are on the honor system.
Please place your fee in the box,
if no park sticker.
Season passes may be obtained ...

I got out of the car and walked to the other side of the booth. Yes, the sign was there, too. If the booth wasn't manned, where had the old man came from? How had he known I'd left my boys? And... there had never been an arbor with a swing there before!

Today, it still remains a mystery. Even so, I left that beach knowing I was not alone in my struggles. I could handle whatever life handed me.

Those boys are now grown with families and struggles of their own. I, now, watch their lives, which reflect the hope and faith of mine learned one day, long ago on a rainy beach. I am content as I await the day when I will see those compassionate eyes once again.

FIRST BLESSING / BLESS AN ANGEL
(for Sr. Mary)
By Vincent Maher

The radiant smile,
utterly unafraid of transcendence,
a toothy grin that stretches
thin lips across a face crossed
by interstates of 93 years
lit by still lapis eyes
made larger by pewter framed
granny glasses that only people like her
seem to find

Bony, blue veined hands,
paper thin skin covering gently
articulated bones that belong
in a medical sketchbook --
thanks sprung from her core
that as she caresses you she is...
touching the Lord.

her wings are spoked wheels framing
a padded chariot
skinny, stilled legs slip
foolhardy attempts to shackle body
as soul soars to primordial music
played by Spiritsong
dancing amidst sidereal dust

She whispered "I claim your first blessing"
As she bestowed Easter words
Straight into my heart:
"Peace. Peace be with you."
My heart echoed:
"See you in Heaven."

NEVER GIVE UP
By Vanessa A. Jackson Austin

If your brook has all dried up
And you feel as though you cannot cope
Because you are without hope,
Never Give Up.
If your way seems too bumpy
With all the twists and turns
And there is no one who appears concerned,
Never Give Up.

If therein emerges a dead end
And as you look around
There is much trouble to be found
Never Give Up.
For if you just call on me
in your days of trouble
I will strengthen you and
Give you much courage.
I will never give up on you
For I am loyal, honest, and forever true.

A THING OF BEAUTY
By Deb Sherrer

Poised on the edged of an indigo forest framed by a purplish-black night sky, she entered a clearing. There was a gathering ahead and, as she drew closer, she saw a circle of people banded together around a bonfire, then fanning out in a spiral. Each person carried a tin lantern that swayed in their grasp and on each one: star, moon, sun, and flower shapes were illuminated through the small pinpricks of light flowing out.

At first it was difficult to see the people's faces, but the more closely she looked, she began to recognize them. There was Mrs. K., her fourth grade teacher, whose kindness had flowed to every child in the classroom, but was remembered with the greatest clarity by those most hungry. And there was Ms. B., her high school English teacher, who had taught her about racism, sexism, and feminism and a world beyond rural Vermont. She recognized the dark, wiry hair of Marty and Jim's strawberry-brown head and wry smile, friends from her 20s whom she hadn't seen in years.

The inner circle held those she loved most dearly: Jason, her husband; Lesley, her best friend from college; Joe, her forever friend; and her soul sisters: JoD, Jennifer, Lorelei; as well as her beloved daughters, dressed in lavender and rose capes.

And while she was still uncertain what was unfolding, her breath caught when she recognized herself, dressed in a long, flowing, white gown, with a crown of yellow spray roses and blue forget-me-nots placed upon her head. From a tar black pit, objects were being extracted, acknowledged, and then thrown into the bonfire. Each was linked to some experience in her life that had evoked suffering, had required healing, and here, at long last, was the public acknowledgment. What was horrific, unspeakable, or seemingly too far in the past, and yet, at times, still achingly painful, could finally be laid to rest.

The next object removed from the pit was a black onyx ring, mounted in gold, with an engraved knight on the stone. It was his ring – the one who had pulled her out of bed in the middle of the night by the head of her hair and a handful of nightgown when she was eight years old. He had screamed at her how terrible she was, the alcohol on his breath spewing out with each hateful word. Then he had shoved her toward her mother, telling her to explain what was wrong because he couldn't trust himself.

Her mother had pathetically, drunkenly, shown her the infinitesimal scratches on the aluminum runners of the sliding shower doors. Her mistake was that she had been standing up on the runners to see herself in the mirror over the sink, because she was too little to do it without a stool and one wasn't provided. She was told to apologize to him and when she did, he struck her across the face, her small body flinging backwards toward the bed. His words to her mother afterwards, "I could have killed her," hung dangerously in the air, as her body shook underneath the covers.

She couldn't say in retrospect if sleep ever came again that night, but she did remember the next two to three days of torturous punishment, the demeaning comments and criticisms at every turn, the remarks that were meant to wound and isolate, make her feel small and dirty and unlovable -- which they did. It was one horrible memory, just one of many that she had learned to hold and live with.

The ring was passed around the inner circle and then raised to the heavens. The vision of herself in the circle was asked if she wished to hold it. When she declined, her oldest friend, Joe, came forward to throw it into the fire. When the ring disappeared, the light grew brighter and a small star emerged from the flames heading for the sky, while stardust filtered gently down to the ground, lighting a patch of earth.

This was a ceremony of transformation; she understood it fully now, and she sat on the ground to watch. But no sooner had her body settled upon the dew soaked grasses, then she too had been transformed; no longer the onlooker, but the participant, the folds of her white dress whispering softly as she moved, cleansing her with their beauty and elegance.

It had never been about her, she realized. It had been about so many other things: unresolved World War II trauma, child abuse, inadequate parenting, and unquenchable rage. But it had *felt* like it was about her. Like somehow if she could have done things differently or right, somehow could have been more lovable, it never would have happened. She would have been loved and safe. Her mother wouldn't have neglected and abandoned her in such devastating ways. This is what the child had told herself, because this is all children know. But now she could see it with other eyes, freeing eyes. *It was never about me.*

And so she went to the pit and withdrew a chalkboard. She wrote these words upon it in large print and showed it to all that were present. There was a great silence, as people turned toward her, moving their heads in quiet acknowledgement, while lifting their lanterns skyward. A murmur grew in the crowd, tears flowed freely down peoples' faces, an acknowledgement of the place where everyone's suffering intersects.

A slow chant began, "It was never about you and your essential goodness. Remember this always." She flung the chalkboard into the fire, to which another star was given birth, and stardust filtered down, a gift of healing remembrance and grace. The ceremony continued until the ground was covered with white-gold stardust and the sky glowed with the breath of newly forged stars. And her healing was complete. A thing of beauty mined from the darkness.

THANK YOU FOR THIS DAY, LORD
By Judy Kirk

Thank you that at 69 almost 70
I can be so excited about a day that
I can barely wait for it to begin.
And it's not just because I'm alive
and healthy and well fed with a roof over my head.
It's because I'm alive and doing.
Today I'm going to teach a class about
writing. Oh Lord, this is my passion,
both the writing and the teaching.
It isn't leading people from sin to redemption,
nor cutting into flesh to stop a cancer,
or taking that first step on the moon.
But it's an honorable passion, Lord.
When people write, their souls spill out,
splash like raindrops on the reader
and hearts can be healed,
at least mended with the assurance
that there are others who have
felt the same pain, or joy
or disappointment.
Oh Lord, thank you for this day
and for the days
there is no excitement
or promise or rainbows
for it makes this day
all the sweeter.

IN EXCELSIS DEO
By Precious McKenzie

At her father's house they celebrated the new life growing inside of her. It was there, in her childhood home, the women of her father's family visited her for the first time. She saw their shadows mingling amongst them. Shadows of women she had never known, sitting among the living. They were smiling. There were so many of these shadow women—her grandmother, her sisters and their mothers and sisters. How they smiled. Her father's brother, a large round-faced reverend, nodded and directed her toward the shadow women. He saw them, too.

She followed the shadow women down the hall. When they were alone, in her childhood bedroom, these women presented her with four glass jars and a small, potted evergreen tree. She thought it was a Christmas tree. Three of the jars were filled with smooth, polished beads: pink beads in one jar and ivory beads in the last two.

She opened the lid on the jar that held the pink beads. Each bead was connected by a fine link of silver. As she turned each bead round in the palm of her hand, a name would appear on the surface of the bead. Names she could not pronounce, names she had not heard, ancient names from before—names of her father's mothers and their sisters and their mothers and their sisters.

The jars of ivory beads were filled much the same. Names of women appeared as she slowly lifted the strands of beads from the jars. Verses of scripture also floated from the ivory beads: verses that she had heard or perhaps read in church years and years ago.

The last jar contained a dark, thick liquid. As she lifted the jar's lid, this liquid glistened but moved little. From some forgotten recess inside of her, she recognized this ancient gift. Myrrh: a gift of hope and healing; a gift for one who is very much loved.

The shadow women were hovering around her and still smiling upon her. She returned their smiles and thanked them for their gifts. As the shadow women departed, they sang "Gloria, In excelsis deo, Gloria" with the syllables stretched to their fullest and most poignant. She felt waves of comfort and peace wash over her unborn child. Her husband came to stand by her side. Enchanted, she could not articulate what had occurred in her father's house.

A LESSON I LEARNED TODAY
By Molly Tienda

Driving down the street a man I would see
Dirty all over and no shoes on his feet
A bundle in a grocery bag is what he calls his own
A hot hard cement place under a bridge is what he calls home
A man once intelligent and now lost in place
He once had friends and family, they once knew his name and face
He now walks the streets in search of food and a place to rest
Every day is a mission to survive and to find food is his quest
Every day I would pass him and give him no thought
But today was quite different, my attention he had caught
I looked at this ragged man thinking about what he had lost
What had happen or what had he done to have to pay at this terrible cost
I pray to God in silence to help him make it through this day
To help him find a warm meal and a safe place to stay
Not to take things for granted is what I learned today
Because they can easily be given and they can easily be taken away

AN INTIMACY OF MATTER
By Sandra Berris

I know the sparkling that heavens the earth,
we saw it,
more than that, bore witness to strange phenomenon:
together on the edge of lawn this November day standing in a half-circle
of four, while Lee, eldest daughter, on the end
of our blood-bonded curve,
scoops her hand into ashes and tiny bones
kept dark and airless for nearly a year, the remains
patterned with hand-painted orange and pink flowers,
keeper of earthly remains,
and like a brain sifting memories
her hand gathers sorrow
and rises like a tree and opens
in loving gesture as if a wave
releasing ash to wind,
her hand empty now
as we each take turns touching the past, release fragments
of frenzied laps around the house,
singing along with an alto sax,
sitting in sun-slants across the hardwood floor,
spinning in dance for a crumb,
until the final handful of all that was and is
floats on wind and at this precise moment
we see heaven's sparkle,
dormant ash on air, magic dust, flash like snow and stars and also
at this precise moment
all the neighbors' dogs begin barking,
their conundrum catching our startled belief.

CHRISTENED FROM ON HIGH
By Linda O'Connell

The one thing that 21-year-old Laney had wanted more than anything, since she was a teenager, was to leave her parent's house and be on her own. Here she was, thousands of miles from her Midwest home, married to a soldier, feeling lonely and very isolated living in an Alaskan wilderness town where a small herd of buffalo tramped down the gravel road on their nightly forage to the woods. Their pounding hooves rattled the only piece of artwork on the wall, a cheap dime store print - some unknown artist's rendition of Jesus, whose eyes she could not hide from no matter where she was in the room. Every time she looked at her sleeping baby, she looked at the picture and sent a silent thank you heavenward. Laney was deeply in love –with Hannah.

Winter darkness had begun to wrap itself around the far north town like a black woolen shawl. Each day it enveloped the 500 residents earlier and earlier. Today it was pitch dark by 3:30 p.m. As Laney prepared another ground beef dinner, she heard the rumble of approaching school buses; their headlights pierced the darkness. She looked out the window for Polaris, the bright North Star. It was the one she'd wished upon since she was a child, and tonight she was going to wish as hard as she could that Hank would agree to her suggestion. There was a complete absence of light. On cloudless nights, brilliant stars and moonlight compensated for the lack of street lamps. Normally the aurora borealis looked as though a child had splashed luminous pastel paints across the sky, and the stars looked so close, Laney thought she could reach right up and pluck one. She felt close to God when she looked at the night sky; the twinkling stars were truly one of His gifts. Late at night when she felt lonely and missed her mom, she walked outside and looked at the constellations. It comforted her to realize that she and her mother were both viewing the same stars.

Laney's sadness had been overwhelming earlier that morning. When she ripped another page off the calendar, September's autumnal picture reminded her of the colorful giant sugar maples back home. Not at all like the woods up here, she thought as she gazed across the road at the cluster of little scrub cedars and skinny evergreens. The growing season was so short; none of the trees grew large in diameter. Not one of them had a trunk big enough to hide behind if a moose lumbered nearby as she was wandering the narrow paths.

Before the baby was born, Laney walked in the woods and rested her hands upon her swollen belly. She wondered aloud what it would be like to be a mother, and she asked God to give her a healthy baby. He'd blessed her with Hannah, now four months old.

Laney was anxious to get home and show Hannah off to friends and family. Hank's tour of duty wouldn't be over for another six weeks, and the days seemed to drag. "I'd be taking the baby for an evening stroll about now, stopping to talk to neighbors if we were home," she thought. Tears flowed silently down her cheeks as she prepared dinner. "I'm so miserable," she said aloud to Hannah stirring in her bouncy seat.

Hank mumbled, "What are you so unhappy about?"

"Oh nothing; must be hormones." Laney averted eye contact with Hank, and Jesus. One of them already knew she was a liar. Her life was a mess. Here she was, so far from home and family, unhappily married to a pessimistic husband, and she had no support system. Their daughter lay in a used wooden port-a-crib with mattress slats that occasionally dropped to the floor. Laney retrieved a diaper from the bookshelf which substituted as the baby's dresser. Hank had gotten it from the barracks and painted it blue, hoping for a boy.

"We'll be going home soon, and you'll have your own furniture and room," Laney murmured to Hannah. "Since I was a little girl I've dreamed of you; I can't wait for you to meet your grandmas," she cooed.

"Hank, what are we going to do about having the baby baptized?" Laney asked point blank, although she'd rehearsed her speech all day.

"You know how I feel about religion. I'm not getting up early every Sunday morning to hear some storyteller."

Hank had no religious upbringing. Laney, on the other hand, had attended Sunday school classes as a child and was baptized in the same church as her grandparents, parents, aunts, uncle and cousins. When she was a preteen, her parents divorced, but she continued to attend church, a number of churches actually. Sometimes she went to mass with her girlfriend, sometimes she went to charismatic services of another denomination, and other times her parents insisted she watch televangelists. She was confused by the differences of each denomination. But she did believe in God's message of salvation. She tried to live her life according to the Golden Rule.

61

Laney looked into Hannah's little face as she laid her in the crib and wound up her mobile. She'd been worried all day about what her neighbor, Sheila, had told her that morning as they rocked their newborn daughters and munched English muffins.

"You have to get your baby baptized soon, or you know what will happen if you don't?"

"What?" Laney asked, curiously.

"You've never heard of baby limbo? If your baby dies before she's baptized, she'll never get to heaven; her soul will float around in limbo for eternity."

Laney didn't know what to believe. Religion was so confusing. She felt the urgency to get Hannah baptized. She pleaded with Hank.

"Let's just choose one of the four churches in town this Sunday. The denomination doesn't matter. I really would like to have the baby baptized before we fly home."

"I'm not listenin' to some do-gooder tell me how to live my life." Hank was adamant. Laney lifted Hannah from her crib and placed the sleeping baby in her daddy's arms.

"Hank, please, she's an innocent little soul. I want her to be christened."

Hank looked at his daughter. "Alright," he said with a frown. "I'll go to church this once, but I'm not going to sit in a hard pew for hours, and don't expect me to sing," he grumbled.

Laney looked happily at Jesus' picture above the sofa; she could have sworn he winked one of his roving eyes. She was overjoyed. On Sunday they dressed in their finest; Laney wrapped Hannah in a fluffy pink blanket and walked to the nearest rural church. Hank didn't trust anyone, not the parish members who welcomed him warmly and certainly not the pastor who invited them into his study when they asked about baptism. The pastor explained that in order to baptize their daughter, they'd have to join the church and tithe.

"If I could afford ten percent of my pay, we'd be eatin' more than hamburger and canned tuna fish seven days a week." Hank stood up and walked out. Laney shrugged her shoulders, embarrassed. She wanted to say that she was more than willing to eliminate a pound or two of red meat and smelly fish on her plate each week in order to put an offering in the collection plate. She'd do anything to have her baby christened. She apologized to God's servant for her husband's behavior, and walked into the small chapel and seated herself. Hank sat beside her. Hannah snuggled in Laney's arms during the sermon. As the congregation stood to sing a hymn, Hannah awoke bright-eyed and smiled a big toothless grin. Laney propped her over her shoulder. The familiar hymn was one Laney remembered from childhood, and she sang it with gusto. Baritone and soprano voices blended and rose above the organ music. Hannah raised her little head high and sang - yes she sang - in her little four month old cooing baby voice, she sang her praises too.

"Do you hear her singing?" Laney jabbed Hank in the ribs.

He nodded, closed mouth, counting the minutes until he could leave. The pastor motioned for the congregation to be seated and asked them to bow in silent prayer. Laney settled the baby in her lap, bowed her head in reverence and spoke to God from her heart. "Lord, I am so confused by all the world's religions, but I do believe in You, and I ask You on this day to forever protect Hannah. I promise to teach her about You, Lord. Please baptize my baby and accept her into your kingdom."

A tear slipped down Laney's cheek. She wanted so badly to walk to the font, dip her fingertips in the holy water and sprinkle it on Hannah's forehead. She knew it wasn't possible, but she did believe in her heart, that with God, all things were possible. She knew that He had heard her prayer and this gave her a deep sense of comfort. The congregation recited the Lord's Prayer and as the service concluded, the pastor made the sign of the cross, "In the name of the Father, the Son and the Holy Spirit...."

Laney's heart was heavy as she wrapped the baby snuggly in her blanket. As the young family walked home from the little church, she couldn't believe it; a light misty drizzle began to fall. It hadn't rained in months. It never rained this late in the year. Laney looked up at the heavens, opened the baby's blanket and exposed Hannah's head.

"What in the heck are you doing?" Hank raised his voice.

Laney smiled, and said softly, "Hank, it's *what in God's name* I'm doing." She made the sign of the cross on the baby's wet forehead and thanked the Lord for her unexpected blessing and His mysterious ways.

UNCONDITIONALLY
by Bernice Angoh

At your best, at your worst
you always will be special to me
when you fall, when you weep
I'm never too far away from you
on my shoulder you can always lean
Let the tear drops fall, I will catch them
(I'll make every one of them into a pearl necklace)
Come to me
Let me share your worries
I'll always be nearby
To remind you of how wonderful you are
What no one sees
Is what we both know
You're vulnerable, human, incomplete
I'm willing to step aside, as hard as it may be
Willing to let go, if that's what you need
(Time and space to grow)
To be the best you can ever be
So that the world, can also get to see
What it is, that I see in you
Sunshine, magic, heaven, beautiful you
The road ahead awaits you
Step into your best shoes, put them to use
Let your every step turn to gold
(Watch yourself fly)
And when the darkness crawls in like it sometimes does
let the smile on your face be because
you know someone, somewhere, loves you
and loves you unconditionally too.

THE LAUGH'S ON ME
By Frances Seymour

I am convinced that God allows me to do some really stupid things in order to teach me valuable life lessons. Here's my newest revelation.

You see, I had this huge patch of gray hair right in the front and top of my head. Why, my daddy never had that much gray hair when he was seventy years old. Of course, he never had that much hair either. But that's beside the point.

Last week I made the decision to put light brown color on my hair to cover the gray. I was excited about this decision. As soon as I got off of work on Friday, I rushed to Wal-Mart to pick up the additives needed to complete the assignment I'd mapped out for myself. Once the color was applied and I looked in the mirror. I felt almost sick. It was too dark, I thought.

My husband came in from working out of town and said, "What did you do to your hair?" I said, "Oh I decided to cover the gray." He said, "Looks like you did. It's a little dark, don't you think? It looks good though," he quickly inserted. Of course filtering this comment with my pink hearing aid, depression quickly begins to settle in. Can you relate?

Next morning, I was still feeling the negative effects of my new color so I decided to visit a friend. She said nothing about my new look — no comment. My daddy used to say, "If you can't say something good, just don't say anything at all." I figured my friend's dad taught her these same words of wisdom and so my gloomy feeling hung tight throughout the weekend.

This morning my husband loaded up and left out for his job in South Carolina and I sat down to pen my thoughts on paper during my quiet time. I opened my laptop to my 'Catch of the Day' devotional by John Fisher and this is what jumped out at me. I have to tell you that I've been praising God in response.

"If you can't laugh at yourself sincerely and often, then you are taking yourself way too seriously!" I pondered this comment over and again until finally, I could sincerely laugh at myself. I realized too, that God allowed me to color my hair so I would come to this same conclusion. He does not want us to take ourselves so seriously. We are fallible human beings and to think that we are or could possibly be any more than that is ridiculous.

We are going to do some things on occasion that even surprise ourselves. Get over it! Laugh about it and move on. It's not the end of the world and God is not through with us yet. So take a good hard look at yourself today. Are you taking yourself too seriously as I apparently was? Then learn to laugh at yourself too, sincerely and often.

INTERVENTION
By Carolyn T Johnson

what if it *is* cancer?
what if it has spread?
what if I have to have chemo?
what if I'm hospitalized for a week?

my mind tumbles,
my thoughts run rampant,
my heart bangs against my chest,
my *what if's* drive me to distraction,
my dad's legacy reaches out from the grave

falling into the abyss
the unknown consumes me,
takes me to the darkest depths,
makes me walk in the shadow of death.

Then
through the overcast sky,
through the leafy tree branches,
through the Celtic cross in the window,
through the ray of sunshine, comes my answer.

the shadow of a simple cross
floats over my heavy heart
and as quickly as it comes,
it goes,
leaving me at peace,
knowing everything
will be
alright.

SNAPSHOT OF DESTINY
By Lynn C. Johnston

Some moments in life are so powerful that they are seared in your memory like a photograph. Years later, we can still recall where we were, what we were doing and how we felt as easily as if it had happened yesterday. Sometimes those moments change your life forever; sometimes they become a snapshot of your destiny.

On Saturday, September 25, 1999, I had one of those life-changing moments.

I had woken up early in hopes of having some "quiet time" with a hot cup of freshly-brewed coffee before my 4-year-old son arose and had me off and running for the rest of the day. As I impatiently watched the coffee dripping slowly into the pot, an intense feeling drifted over me. It was a familiar feeling I had had for much of my life – it was time to write again.

Ever since I was in middle school, I had been a writer in one form or another. I started out writing a soap opera with my best friend in seventh grade. We were avid fans of "General Hospital" and began believing similar storylines could apply to our teachers and friends. We were convinced that the platinum blonde science teacher with green-tinged hair was really a cleverly disguised Martian planning to take over the world. And, of course, the pregnant social studies teacher must have become so only after having a torrid, one-night stand with the married English teacher.

Over the years, my writing eventually progressed. I wrote short stories and personal essays before becoming a journalism minor in college. As a reporter and managing editor of the college newspaper, my writing had now become based in fact, not fiction. It had also become an addicting hobby. If I went without writing for more than a week or two, a suffocating frustration would envelope me until I finally released it through writing; it was like being trapped in an itchy sweater that could only be removed by putting pen to paper. On this quiet September morning, it was clear to me what I needed to do. But what would I write? I did not have a subject to satiate this need.

As I sipped my coffee, a voice bellowed in my head. It wasn't aloud, but its message was crystal clear. It told me to write a poem. Out of all the writing genres I had attempted, poetry had not really been one of them.

"But I don't write poetry," I said silently in my head.

The voice responded in a manner reminiscent of Tyler Perry's "Madea" character – sassy, feisty and impossible to ignore: "I don't care, honey," she chided. "That's your problem. I'm a poem. If you don't write me as a poem, I won't come out."

I was stunned. Where was this coming from?

As I stood there, the voice added her postscript: "By the way, it has to be uplifting and inspirational too."

I stared into my coffee cup confused over what just happened. Had I just been visited by a celestial force conveying God's plan for me, or had the milk I added to my coffee cup been spiked with psychotropic drugs, causing me to have delusions?

Not wanting to disobey this mysterious voice, I began writing poetry that weekend. It took eight hours to write and polish my poem, but by Sunday night I was finally done... and the itchy sweater of pent up creativity had been removed. My poem, "I Love You" was born; a poem about standing on that fine line between love and friendship.

Over the next few months, I found myself writing more and more poetry – this time without all the psychic theatrics.

As my confidence grew, I began sharing my poems with family and friends, including my elderly grandmother living in a nursing home in Florida. Our relationship up to that point had been strained. We never had the close relationship that grandmothers and granddaughters often had. But after she started reading my poems, something changed.

She told me how much she loved my poetry, and how much she wished my deceased grandfather was still here to read it too. Unbeknownst to me, he loved poetry. In fact, she kept an old college textbook that he cherished called "It Can Be Done" by Morris and Adams. In it, he had marked his favorite poems and passages.

What made it all the more astounding to me is that it was all uplifting and inspirational poetry. There wasn't a sad, morose or depressing thought in the whole book. As she gave it to me, I was overwhelmed with this passion I had come to share with my grandfather. How is it that I never knew this about him? And when did he become a sassy, Black woman?

All I had really known was that he was the consummate company man who had spent his life working at Nabisco. He had earned the nickname "Cookie Man" by bringing us packages of cookies in his suitcase – always exuding the same zeal as an Italian mother arriving with homemade lasagnas. In the 17 years we shared before his passing, I never knew this side of him.

As I read through the book, I felt a new connection to my grandparents and to my destiny as a poet. I realized that my experience that fateful September morning wasn't lactic poisoning after all; it was a divine force designed to link me to my grandfather and start me down a new path of spiritual and emotional healing for me and the lives of my readers. It's a snapshot of my destiny that I will always remember.

DREAM HIGH
By Kimberly Alfrey

Dream high atop Rich Mountain
Allow the breeze to blow your hair
Reach out for the sights beyond you
Without a care

With each breath
Dare to believe you can
Embrace the hidden glimpses of shades of gray
Dreaming even bigger than you dared

As the sun rises on your tomorrow
Look boldly forward
Reach for the highest mountain
Daring the valley to give way to hope

Upon the newfound wings of dreams
Ride the winds of change
Challenging them to go your way
Embracing every turn with resolve
~Dreaming the dream of the dreamer

IT'S A MATTER OF ATTITUDE
By Robert D. Fertig

An old man slowly shuffled up to the speaker's platform to make one of his final speeches. His audience was the graduating class of Eton College, outside of London. In a deep, measured, mellifluous voice, he spoke but eight words: "Never, never, never, never, never, never give up." Then, ever so slowly, Sir Winston Churchill shuffled off stage. Those eight words can be your base rock for survival over adversity; they are mine.

Three other words, equally chiseled into my being, completely changed my point of view and perhaps will change yours. They are my mantra, my bench mark for living. From the final words of the third act aria, *Nessun Dorma*, Giacomo Puccini's <u>Turandot</u>: "*All' alba vincero! Vincero!* **Vincero!** (At dawn I shall win! I shall win! **I shall win!**)" Never would I, never will I, ever settle for anything less than succeeding over adversity. Never permit adversity to win!

<u>Nessun Dorma</u> has been sung by all of the world's great operatic tenors. The first concert of the Three Tenors was held in Rome. It concluded with <u>Nessun Dorma</u> sung by the three tenors. Everyone at the concert knew that one of the three tenors, Jose Carreras, had gone through his own personal fight of surviving cancer. He had received painful bone marrow transplants to conquer the disease and knows all to well the meaning of *vincero*. The young, Italian operatic tenor superstar, Andrea Bocelli, also sings <u>Nessun Dorma</u> at his concerts. I am certain that <u>Nessun Dorma</u> has special meaning for him, too. Bocelli is blind.

These words cannot be typed or even read without tears for each time that I went into cancer surgery those words were firmly implanted in my mind, in my heart, in my soul and into the very core of my being. During the past decades I have gone in for cancer surgery three times, and have given up my left kidney, gall bladder, more than half of my rectum and colon and the prostate – the last time facing twenty to one odds. "I shall win!" was my all consuming thought. A few years later, I was cursed with cancer once again. No matter, I thought, *Vincero*. I shall win. And did!

Physicians, hospitals, belief in the Almighty, Jesus Christ or homeopathy cures, all can and do perform miracles. Individually, or collectively, they can do only just so much. In the final analysis, it is entirely up to the person inflicted with the disease or any adversity to instill into self, "Never, never, never, never, never, never give up!"

These words, and too many other close encounters with the grim reaper, have created an attitude of always being positive no matter what the negative situation may be, always - no exceptions - seek something positive out of it. Feeling sorry for self, exponentially increases the personal burden and potentially creates a "loser attitude."

We have the power to change our lives. We only need to give ourselves permission. In doing so, we enrich not only ourselves, but all of those around us. The results of changing our expectations, wants, needs and desires will prove to be nothing short of amazing. Find a window of opportunity when fighting any disease, pain or adversity.

If you or a loved one has been told that you or they have cancer, remember this: it is not necessarily a death sentence! A negative attitude will assist that point of view. You, or they, must realize that a positive attitude, (*Vincero!*) can and will bring you through near impossible odds. Please believe me, I have been there and now I am here writing this for you.

Seek Your Window of Opportunity.

ALONE AT 1 A.M.
By Ysabel de la Rosa

The storm close
The wind wild
The radio crackling
The television dead
No reports
Only sounds
in the wind-whipped dark:
metal scrapes metal
as the roof next door
comes unhinged and
a moan makes its way
through the attic
Blanketed
I huddle
I listen
I wait
yet
I will not
fear
nor will I
dread
for Thou, yes,
Thou art with me,
even as the storm is close,
even as the wind grows wild,
Thou art with me.
Amen.

NOW I'LL DANCE
By Lyn Halper

This is a story about how I went from being a cripple to becoming a *tanguera* – a woman who dances tango. It is a story of how I dragged myself up from a life of pain and despair to one of joy and accomplishment. It is a story about the strong and abiding assistance I had along the way.

It begins in the summer of 2007, when my days were occupied with husband, grown children and friends, after my retirement as a psychologist and professor of World Religions. Much of our time was spent going to the movies, dining in trendy restaurants, and shopping, shopping, shopping. We were adding a kitchen/great room to our house and were caught up with architectural plans and interior design. Maybe, the life I describe is not uncommon for people our age, or more likely, it was superficial and vapid. Certainly, the writing was on the wall: it was the calm before the storm – something was about to happen.

I was noticing in the mornings a stiffness in my legs. When I asked my friends if they experienced this too, nearly all said, yes, and that it was common at our age. This reassured me, and I continued to ignore that it was growing worse week by week. By the end of the summer, our new room was completed – it was everything we hoped, though the pleasure was overshadowed by my physical condition. At summer's end, my feet were burning, my hands aching, and my right arm was too weak to throw off the covers. Even more astonishing, my legs were buckling as I climbed the stairs.

At my first visit to the internist, he said, "I don't want to alarm you, but you might have rheumatoid arthritis. Call me after the weekend; I'll have the results of the blood tests by then." Back home, I felt numb as I told my husband what the doctor had said. He shook his head. "It seems unlikely. We all get aches and pains as we age."

"No," I said, "Something is terribly wrong."

I knew little about the condition and began to research. RA was an autoimmune disease that attacked the muscles, tendons, and bones at the joints of the body, moving rapidly from one joint to another, causing pain, stiffness, muscle weakness and fatigue. It was also known to attack the internal organs of the body. It was progressive. There was no cure.

If I wasn't scared before, after reading, I was heartsick. We headed off late Friday afternoon to our daughter's college for parent's visiting weekend. While I was happy to see her, it was a weekend in hell as I tried, unsuccessfully, to keep my mind off my body. On Saturday night, I popped my last Advil for the day and got into bed. I lay there a long while staring into the dark, thinking dire thoughts, fighting back feelings of panic. My mind jumped around, searching for *anything* to anchor me. I felt I stood at the edge of an abyss and would soon tumble into its depths.

Then, as if prompted by some primal instinct, I did something I hadn't done in years. I closed my eyes and took a deep breath "Please," I said, "be with me. I need Your help." The sound of the traffic outside our hotel window and the beating of my heart seemed to grow quiet. I let go a deep sigh and fell asleep.

When morning came, I opened my eyes with the feeling that an event had occurred. I lay still, and sure enough, a vivid dream was in my mind. I grabbed the hotel stationery pad and pen and wrote quickly:

I'm in my house, only it isn't my house, it has turned into a store. Salesmen are grinning at me with wide false smiles. Although I don't want to, I have to leave this house for another one. The house I am in now is dreary and gray and in the living room is a fireplace with a tin façade covered with dirt and grime. I wander around and come to a door. When I open the door, I am in a bedroom that is clean and newly painted with white walls and modern furniture and sun streaming in though the windows.

My training in psychology suggested that the "house" was my body. That it had "turned into a store," reflected my sense of guilt for being heavily invested in material things. The bright sunny room at the end of the dream could be dismissed as nothing more than wish-fulfillment. Yet, my knowledge of religions and spiritual practices told me this was a Big Dream, one that offered an esoteric reason for my health dilemma, and prophetically, illustrated an outcome. Back home, I pasted the hotel stationery with its scrawled dream into my journal. Over the next several weeks I read and re-read it ceaselessly. The more I pondered it, the more convinced I became that the dream had import.

I was now running from one doctor to another, wanting each one to "save" me and feeling bitter disappointment when their remedies did little to alleviate the condition.

My older son said, "Mom, you're going in circles. Take responsibility – get a trainer and work on your muscles."

I felt he was right and found a physical therapist. His regime was painful for muscles that hadn't been used and now were compromised by an illness. In fact, the exercises were exacerbating the condition. It was now two months since the diagnosis and it was clear I was getting worse. I hadn't the strength to get out of a chair or turn on the car ignition. There was a marked limp.

One night I went into my darkened bedroom to think about my situation. Things looked bad, but there had to be a solution. I just needed to reason it out. Medical practitioners had not helped, but surely there were other options. I thought hard and kept coming up against a brick wall. My husband was out for the evening and the house felt empty. I no longer knew what to do. Perhaps there was nothing to do but give up. If destiny wanted to destroy me, so be it. I sat slumped on the bed, palms open, admitting defeat. That's when a feeling came over me that things would change.

The next week, quite unexpectedly, the right doctor appeared – a noted RA specialist, and his treatments began to take effect. Soon, I was strong enough to leave physical therapy and transition to a gym. At the local fitness center I plodded along on the treadmill at a snail's pace; but at least, I was moving. I thought more intently about my spiritual life and realized I had let it atrophy just like my body.

That evening, I went rummaging around our basement till I found my old copy of Norman Vincent Peale's, *The Power of Positive Thinking*. His message was simple, clear and direct. When we saturate our minds with positive thoughts bolstered by prayer, amazing things can happen. Each night in bed, I visualized myself walking, climbing stairs, getting stronger. My inner life was coming alive; dreams came like signposts showing my progress or regression along the way; most were reassuring. I was doing better at the gym, using machines to build upper and lower body strength. I could now climb stairs and my walk was becoming more natural. One day it came to me: my goal was too narrow. Why work to get back to the place I'd been? Why not go beyond it! I recalled something I'd always wanted to do – Argentine tango: the complex dance that demanded agility and precision to execute *ganchos* and *boleos* – dozens of difficult steps that placed pressure on the body and the legs, but was magnificent to see and perform.

By summer's end, my husband and I were taking lessons at a local studio. At first I worried whether my knees would withstand the punishment of two-hour lessons, intense practice, *malongas* – tango dance events – but somehow, it was never a problem. I soon discovered there was a spiritual element to the dance: the opening move was called *salida*, meaning "exit." To begin, you left real time and entered cosmic time. When dancing, I felt connected to a transcendent reality. Buoyed up by the music and the sound of the *bandoleon*, I knew what it was to be happy. After a year, I could execute the most intricate steps.

Sometimes I look back to the time when I couldn't walk, or climb stairs, or rise from a chair. I think of the time when I felt afraid, lost, and in pain. I close my eyes and remember what it was that brought me so long a distance. Then I smile and say, "Yes. Now, I'll dance. "

SHAPES OF SELF
By Amy S. Pacini

When you calmly sit down to pray and quietly meditate
You can clear your mind and silently listen to God's voice
You can hear him telling you to rely on his grace and love
For no matter what is happening in your life
He is always there to guide you
He provides you with comfort and courage
God has carried you through the struggles and difficult times
He can make you stronger and more resilient because of them
These trials can serve as stepping stones to success
Throughout your life
You can learn to conquer your fears
And accept that you are not confined
To the inside lines of your past
For it only marks the point from where you have begun
And shapes who you will be in the years to come
You can move forward in your life with passion and purpose
And cherish the valuable lessons
On your journey towards self-discovery
Which only come from the experiences you endure
For you are a person gifted with strength, talent and beauty
And have the potential to be anybody.

DANCING IN THE RAIN
By Robert B. Moreland

Evening thunderstorm, late in May,
in the darkest times, take your hand.
Smile at freckles, hazel eyes wondering
and dance for hope in the rain.

Is God listening in heaven tonight?
Can He grant yet another wonder?
Hope for the best, plan for the worst,
take my hand, and dance in the rain.

Wish for wine Christ made at Cana,
glance wistfully into your eyes...
Hear the peaceful sighs, resignation,
pray for miracles dancing in the rain.

Oh, sweet reprieve and hope found!
Death sentence stayed for a little while...
Though the path is hard, I am with you,
in heaven we will dance in the rain.

GIVEN PAIN
By Lucy Jane Barnett

It started subtly at first, a dull ache or pinch that never fully formed nor vanished. I was still the same, able to do what I wanted in my usual all-or-nothing way. And then, in a time of joblessness and personal stress, my body seemed to be overwhelmed with pain. I would stumble through days filled with hot, burning muscles, too tired to stand and suddenly falling asleep whenever I stopped moving. It was a haze at first and I can remember crying constantly with pain and fear as I struggled to determine the cause.

Six years ago, it seemed like all the small symptoms that had flitted outside my radar of awareness, converged at once to get my attention. I had left a stable, well-paying job in order to create my own business and things were not working as I had hoped. Like most small businesses, I had limited financing and had been unrealistic with my immediate business goals. While my burgeoning debt was softened by the loveliness of a new relationship, stress turned my stomach tight with tension and kept me restless most nights. At first, I had rational excuses for why my body hurt and all the associated issues. When my arms could no longer manage the labor of shampooing my hair, I knew that I needed to see a doctor.

There were tests, from blood work to mapping my sleep habits and more questions than answers. The only constant was the pain. I was used to doing what needed to be done and I could only rage in frustration at my feelings of helplessness. Months passed, and regardless of medical interventions, I was the same.

Unfortunately, this new me was not who I wanted to be. Every day, I would face relentless patterns of pain, making me cranky and angry at this body that had failed and at the world in general. Soon, I was given a diagnosis of sorts: fibromyalgia. My doctor couldn't give me a cause or a cure; I hobbled from his office, wondering what was next.

I had always fancied myself as a spiritual person, feeling intrinsically connected to my faith and the concept of a benevolent deity. My illness challenged me, causing my faith to waver in the face of feeling punished by my physical limitations, particularly the pain. I martyred myself, trying to find some purpose for being sick and falling short. I was angry, daunted by the idea that the rest of my life would be encapsulated by this struggle. I spent years enraged by the unfairness of it all, faith transformed into a word without meaning. It was like shouting at the ocean, raging against the tide. No matter how fierce my questions, I was mired by forces stronger than me.

It came to a head, late one night as I struggled to stand, swallowing tears in an attempt to deny my pain. I lay back instead and allowed myself to be comforted by the softness of my bed. I felt how it held me, supporting me easily and reflected how certain I was in its constancy. I realized, with the type of sudden clarity that comes rarely, that I had struggled because I was trying to do it on my own. My illness, my pain, my need for help – I had refused to share it fully, with my family, lover, friends or the Divine. I started to do something that I hadn't done since first feeling unwell: I prayed.

"God – my mother, my father, my everything – I need your help. I don't believe you want me to suffer and I refuse to accept this illness or the pain it brings. I will do everything I can to nurture my body back to health but I need you to take my pain from me. I know you will."

I fell asleep almost immediately and woke up later the next morning, brimming with an unshakeable optimism. As I swung my legs out of bed, it took a moment to realize that I had almost imperceptible levels of pain. I actually lay back down, testing to see if I worked properly a second time. The rest of the day was buoyed by my smiles and gratitude as I struggled to accept that my life had changed again, this time for the better.

I won't say that my faith was absolute. My reduction in pain was so substantial, I found myself wondering and questioning how this had happened. But as the days became weeks, then months, and finally years, I accept it joyously. It's difficult to find a doctor who understands my recovery, let alone believes it, but I have faith enough for both of us. I still will have days where I hurt, sometimes badly, but it is rare enough that I no longer doubt I will be mostly well in the future.

In the beginning, I struggled so fiercely being sick, unable to see the point or purpose in my suffering. I understand now that the worst is behind me, what a gift my illness was. I had lived my life, up until that point, happiest to give to others and reluctant to receive in return. I was given pain, not as a burden but as a gift, to learn how to allow other, gentler, gifts to gracefully enter my life. My faith was tested and

82

emerged stronger for the challenge. I know with certainty that it and my love for the divine will float the way hope does. With certainty.

LIMITLESS LOVE
By Connie Arnold

No matter what valley you travel through
In a deep and rugged ravine,
As the burdens of life press upon you,
There's a power on which you can lean.

When overcome with sorrow and pain,
As trials seem to increase,
God's mercy and grace still remain,
Providing comfort and peace.

When your strength fails you before
You can finish what you had begun,
God's power can do so much more
When you pray that His will be done

On God's limitless love you can depend
Throughout the life you are living.
There are no boundaries and no end
To the love God freely is giving.

MARVELOUS MESSIAH
By Amy S. Pacini

He walks beside me along life's undulating sea
He hears every painful cry and merciful plea
He carries my wilted body in his strong arms
And takes me away from anything that harms
He heals my soul with his powerful hand
And leads me to follow in his miraculous plan
He never abandons me or leaves my side
He is always there, he does not hide
Whenever I am afraid,
I gaze up to heaven and pray
I know that everything will be okay
For I trust in his wonderful way
When the storms of life knock me to the ground
He comforts me and does not let me drown
His grace is stupendous and his love never ends
Holy and just is he, God never pretends
In the darkness, he is my glorious light
In the forest, he is a compass of magnificent might
He feels every emotion known to man

He changes my words
From "I can't" to "You can"
There is nothing that he cannot handle
Next to him, no mortal can hold a candle
He lives within the core of our souls
He is always present during each high and low
For God is eternally faithful
And continues to guide us
Wherever we go.

PULLING UP BY MY BOOTSTRAPS
By Glenda Barrett

Having been an independent person my entire life, I was deeply humbled each morning as I sat on the side of the bed and put on my special shoes, one which held a brace for the right leg. A few years ago after recovering from a spinal fusion, I was diagnosed with a neuromuscular disease that affects the peripheral nerves. Since that time, I've had three foot surgeries including two ankle fusions. I now have a brace on my right leg and use a scooter part-time. For someone who had been working two jobs and had to give them up, that is certainly a change.

In the beginning there were times in the morning, I resented having to put the brace on. I hated it along with the ugly, bulky, large shoes! I remember feeling like I'd like to take them out to the trash and burn them, but then I realized they were very expensive. There were other times I felt depressed about having to wear them.

I remember my first trip out in public. I had pulled into the parking lot at the Post Office. I was trying to keep my back straight and get out of the car with the brace on at the same time. I was having a lot of difficulty because the car in the space beside me had parked too close to me. I struggled a bit, and all of a sudden, I felt as if I'd scream at the top of my lungs!

I happened to look up into the other car beside me and noticed an elderly gentleman putting on his oxygen mask. Under my breath I muttered, "Thank you, Lord, I'll keep the brace!"

It is still vivid in my mind the first time I was fitted for the brace. The cheerful man was sitting in front of me wrapping Plaster of Paris around my leg, while small puddles of water fell on the floor leaving circles. He was chatting about the weather, and all of a sudden I felt anger welling up inside of me, and I wanted to lash out at him in some way. Instead, I sat quietly and wondered exactly where this was coming

85

from. I soon realized I was experiencing one of the stages of grief from losing the use of my ankle.

There were other things I had to get accustomed to as well. One day in the grocery store I ran into an acquaintance. Always a friendly girl, she said good naturedly, "Those are the ugliest shoes I've ever seen!" I replied to her, "When it comes to being able to walk and wearing something ugly or not walking, guess which one you will do?" She laughed and went on her way. She meant no harm, but I was still feeling pretty vulnerable.

My doctor at Emory told me, "Glenda, to save your energy, use the scooter when you need it, especially in the grocery stores, where there is a lot of walking."

Like the shoes and brace, I remember thinking, "I'll not ride in that thing; I'm only fifty-years-old." However, it wasn't long, until I found out if I didn't want to be in extreme pain I would ride in it. It took me several tries to sit down in it, but after awhile I could do it. I remember the day I fully realized just how far I'd come with my disability. I was riding through the store with no other thoughts but getting my groceries and was doing a quick job when I rounded a corner and almost ran over another shopper. The man laughed and jumped out of my way. After I apologized, I smiled to myself as I realized I had accepted my disability.

One of the most touching comments I ever received came from a small child about four-years-old. I passed her one day as I was coming out of the computer store. She took one look at my shoes and said in the most innocent voice, "You have pretty shoes?" In the next breath, she said, "Can you fix our computer?" I noticed her mother was following behind lugging their computer to be fixed. I remember thinking what a wonderful world it would be if we were all as accepting as a little child – most of the times the grown-ups only stare.

Once again I accepted the situation, and in the summer I got brave enough to wear a pair of shorts out in public.

It's been several years now since I was diagnosed, and I've had a lot of time to work through some of my grief. Not only tha,t after the constructive foot surgeries, I'm wearing and walking in a regular pair of athletic shoes. Yes, I was able to toss those shoes in the trash!

My disease is incurable and progressive, and I realize there will be other challenges to overcome. To tell you the truth, even though there have been a lot of struggles, I'll have to say it has been the most meaningful time of my life. I know you are raising your eyebrows as you read this, but I'll try to explain. In order to cope with this disease I've been forced to make a lot of changes. I've created a simple life for myself, and strangely enough it agrees with me. I no longer run pell-mell through my life, but I'm grateful for each step, not knowing how long I'll be able to take them. That really makes the difference. On good days I sometimes walk through the grocery store, and I'll hear ladies say, "Don't you hate to go the store?" I tell them, "It is a pleasure to me!"

Not only that, but I now have time for relationships, and I've learned to set boundaries on ones that are not good for me. I feel real sure that these are lessons I wouldn't have learned any other way. Now, as I get dressed each morning I realize the braces taught me some valuable lessons. As I pulled them on, and fastened the Velcro strap around my leg, I realized I'm not in charge of every aspect of my life like I thought. And it is easy for me to say now, "Thank you Lord for another day and another step! You're in charge of my life now." Now that's a mouthful for an independent lady!

ARTISTS

for Denise
By Bruce Dethlefsen

we chase the moon
too hard sometimes
and stumble in the stars
that sparkle always blinds us
we trip and tumble down
we suffocate in stardust
drown in floodlight
and still we recreate
we sing   we write
we dance   we paint
we one more time in space
ourselves remake
return   retune
gracefully we rise again
we're artists
grateful for another dreadful chance
to chase the moon

THE CRIPPLED CROW
By Annette Geroy

Have you ever seen a crippled crow? There was one in our yard some time ago and the image of him trying to hop around stuck with me. He was missing a leg so his movements were very erratic; *hop, lunge, compensate*. His black eyes darted in their sockets, ever anxious to avoid danger. His feathers were mussed and ugly; after all, it is hard to preen when you are off balance. Can you visualize that crippled crow?

That is how I was feeling the year the truth of my childhood sexual abuse began to unravel. I found myself caught up in a fierce struggle. I had begun to experience some healing and freedom, but contemplating the thought of going home for Christmas made me physically ill. I had always tried to do the right thing, and going home for Christmas was one of those things. But, I just could not do it! The anger and pain swirled together with the guilt and anxiety. I was not able to keep my emotions balanced: *hop, lunge, compensate*.

I had talked to my mother and brother years before about having been sexually abused by my father, but they seemed to have forgotten! So I took a huge risk and wrote my mother a letter. I pored over that letter. I asked the Lord to give me honest but gracious words. It was not an easy task because I needed her love and acceptance. I wrote that I had forgiven my father, and her, but my emotions were just too raw to be in that house for Christmas.

I put the letter in the mail with extra postage and a prayer that it would be well received.

She responded in an angry, protective-of-Ann tone that set my heart spinning with hope and expectations. I finally felt I had the protective guardianship of my mother. I was relieved and encouraged.

She asked if she should read the letter I had sent to be placed in my father's casket when he died. At that time he was an invalid in the nursing home. Wanting to maintain this new connection with her I responded, "I don't care if you read it or not. I don't care what you do with it." As the words left my lips, I knew it was a lie. I did care, but I was basking like a favored child in her concern for me. I should have listened to the still small voice whispering words of caution in my ear. Instead, I was afraid that she would misunderstand my motives and withdraw her love, so I remained silent--*hop, lunge, compensate.*

I did not go home for Christmas.

There was a great time of intimacy and fellowship with the Lord throughout the winter, so I was surprised when I hit a dry spell in the spring. I was not anxious or fretting, things were just quiet for a while. As I prayed, I could see in my mind's eye a stack of old boards. It made no sense to me at first. Continuing to pray over a period of several weeks, I could see the Lord building a fence. He and I were on one side of the fence and the rest of the world was on the other side. Behind the fence we played and romped, I sat in his lap and he sang to me; we danced. It was as though I were a young child — His child. It was a heady feeling.

Following an extended illness, my father died on June 8th. I had lost any sense of connectedness to him over the previous year. I had already said my good byes in the letter I had written to him. His passing brought only a final sigh of release.

My mother and brother handled all of the arrangements. Things were under control. The casket had been left open with pictures taken over his lifetime displayed on an easel and propped inside the casket. Since my father was a World War II veteran, the casket was draped with an American flag. A Christian flag and an American Legion flag flanked each end.

I could manage only a cursory glance. I simply stepped away to wait quietly while the rest of the family said their good byes. I vacillated between being distracted by well wishers and trying not to throw up! My daughter edged next to me and whispered, "Mom, where is your letter?" I told her I assumed it was in the casket as I had asked. There was no reason to think my mother would not honor my wishes, yet a nagging fear began to grip my heart.

The morning of the funeral my mother called to remind us to be at the funeral home at 9:00 for the family gathering. That is when I asked her about my letter. She paused then replied, "I tore it up! I tore them both up and threw them in the garbage! You said you didn't care, so I thought it was alright for me to throw them away." I could barely breathe. I hung up the phone, dropped to the floor and began to keen like a wounded animal, howling softly with devastating grief.

That old familiar feeling of abandonment overwhelmed me. My throat was choked with gut wrenching sobs surging up in waves.

The pain was so intense I thought my skin would crack. She tore the letters up and threw them in the garbage? The things I had spent months preparing were nothing but trash. I felt as though she had chosen him over me, once again.

I rushed out of the motel room to find my husband in the parking lot—coffee in hand and a smile on his face. Recognizing my despair from a distance, he ushered me into a white plastic chair near the pool. He quaked as I shared my anguish, then was very still for a while. Finally he said, "Ann, she is still living in denial. I don't think she meant for this to hurt you even though it has. She just cannot deal with the truth."

Like the night shade on a window, I pulled down my mask and survived the next few hours--*hop, lunge, compensate.*

When I was finally home and able to talk with the Lord about my pain, he took me to the strangest place—2 Kings 25:30 *So Jehoiachin put aside his prison clothes and for the rest of his life ate regularly at the king's table. Day by day the king gave Jehoiachin a regular allowance as long as he lived.*

The Lord said, "Ann, you can take off your smelly old prison clothes and join me at the king's table where I have made provision for you, or you can cling to the past and be miserable. The choice is yours."

The first step was to take off my prison clothes. *...put off your old self which is being corrupted by its deceitful desires* (Ephesians 4:22). Rather than the conventional black and white striped uniform, I wore a cloak of desires and expectations that focused on my family. I thought if they would not acknowledge the truth of my abuse that I could not be vindicated. I was holding them accountable. I needed their love and approval, which is not a bad thing, but I was allowing that need to interfere with my relationship with the Lord.

I could see how the Lord had been preparing me for this difficult time. He was waiting for me there, behind the fence. I knew he would let me grieve my losses in his arms. I just had to give up my unholy desires and focus fully on him, knowing that he would meet my every need.

The immediate decision was easy. That tattered old cloak slid from my shoulders as I ran to Jesus, seeking his freedom. I made a choice that day, and Jesus is still fulfilling his promises to me. However, it took me almost two years to learn to walk in freedom—to turn to the Lord as soon as I felt invalidated. I love my family, but their words and actions no longer turn my world upside down. I do not have to *hop, lunge, or compensate* like the crippled crow. Today, I can stand on two feet because of Christ who strengthens me.

This week we will be putting my mother to rest. Her heart has stopped beating. She clung to the only means of self preservation she knew until the end—denial. Yet, by God's grace, I was able to say to her in all honesty, "Mom, I want you to know I hold no ought with you."

SWAN DIVE
By Susan Mahan

I gave my notice at work today
I am leaving a desk job to follow my heart
My heart, which has never paid a bill in its life
says I must write.

It's not like I haven't jumped off cliffs before
I usually close my eyes
hold my nose
and cannonball into the future
hoping for the best

This time, I am poised to swan dive
I will leap off with oomph
My back will be gracefully arched
My eyes will be wide open
and I'll land
like Esther Williams
in a shimmering pool
of
words

RAINDROPS ON A BROKEN WING
By Olga Mancuso

Bless this unlikely soldier
Strengthen what's to come
Comfort me when it's over
You know the sparrows—each one

The lilies dewed and arrayed
Raindrops on a broken wing
Loveliness of faith displayed
Trusting Your promise—within

Disease consumes my body
It can't touch Your servant's soul
The potter shapes the pottery
I don't bear this trial—alone

Change the scarlet robe I wear
Humble me in my weakness
White linen shall clothe me there
Dressed perfectly with—meekness

When the hour turns midnight
I will praise Your holy name
Should I live or should I die
I'm more alive—either way!

THE SMALL VOICE
By Rebekah Crain

I opened my eyes; the ceiling was white, so were the walls. Sergeant Deal, the Ten Miler coach was standing in the corner of the room. "When are we going to go run?" I asked him. He looked down at the floor.

My mom was sitting beside my bed; she looked at me over the bedrail. "Don't you remember? I already told you; you missed the race. You were hit by a car while you were running a few weeks ago."

"We brought back your t-shirt and everyone ran real well." Sergeant Deal looked back at the floor. "We would have run better if you were there though," he added quietly.

I didn't say anything. How could I have missed the race? My thoughts started racing.

Over the next few days I learned that I was hit by a Ford Escort and I had a collapsed lung, a compound leg fracture near my ankle, (which explained the metal sticking out of it, it was called an external fixator) and a subdural hematoma. Apparently I was lucky to get to the hospital as fast as I did. When the doctors opened my skull to relieve the pressure, they found that part of my brain was already dying. They did a partial lobotomy to remove the dead brain matter. Mom was told I would probably not be able to carry a normal conversation again.

"I found your stories from college," my sister told me. "Did you know you wrote one about a girl who almost got hit by a car, but an angel jumped in the way and saved her?"

"Yeah, I modeled that character after me, but where was my angel in real life?"

"Your angel was with you," Mom joined.

"How?" I grumbled, staring at my leg.

"In the EMTs who got there quickly and the doctors who knew exactly what they had to do; miracles happen when everything works in synch."

94

I nodded, not sure I agreed. It was hard to believe there had been a miracle when I was pushed to various therapies in a wheelchair. I was the independent one; I helped people, and I took care of soldiers; now my soldiers were about to deploy without me, and my family was taking care of me. I was being pushed around in a wheelchair when I used to be able to run across the city. It hurt to do anything but sleep; I had headaches ranging from nine to eleven on a ten scale. Yet as I lay in my bed at night and stared at the metal protruding from my leg, a small voice reminded me that I would get better, things would not be like this forever. I prayed that God would let me walk again, but I was lying to myself: walking would never be enough; I needed to run.

Every day I went to my therapies dutifully. I liked my speech therapist, but I got bored trying to figure out where my tongue was supposed to be in my mouth, a thing she patiently coached me to do. I got tired doing the test trying to figure out what random thing was missing in the pictures she showed me. I hated physical therapy; I understood its usefulness, so I told myself to appreciate it, but it hurt to be moving, so I complained to my therapists and some mornings tried to refuse treatment due to head pain. I enjoyed occupational therapy: learning how to navigate myself from my bed to the chair to the toilet and later demonstrating that I could perform daily living functions such as brushing my teeth, while leaning on my crutches. Through each step in the process the voice was there reminding me "this isn't forever." When I got my crutches, it occurred to me that if I was this close to walking, running steps would not be far behind. They are basically the same motion; if I could walk I could run, the small voice urged me.

When I returned to work, the post was a ghost town, most of the units had deployed to Southwest Asia, except those who were pregnant, injured, or otherwise designated to maintain operations at home. As I began work, my leadership treated me like I was fragile; it was then I realized no matter how much better I got, things would never be the same. I wondered what I had done to deserve this punishment. "You're not going to be here forever, different isn't always bad," the voice reminded me.

One of my soldiers passed me in the hall. "It's great to see you Ma'am" she said. "You know there was a time we weren't sure you'd even be able to walk again."

I shook my head. I hadn't heard that part. I had surpassed everyone's ideas of my recovery: I was walking and talking. I was chagrined at feeling sorry for myself.

When I was at my mailbox after work one evening, one of my elderly neighbors was outside; he was hooked up to his oxygen, as usual. He waved and said, "I heard it the day you were hit, it sounded like two cars had run into each other. It's good to see you; you know you're walking proof there is a God." I had no response; I just smiled, nodded, and continued to my apartment wondering. Did my neighbor need the accident? Perhaps I was his message, the voice told me.

I did my job every day, joined a gym and got a personal trainer to help me stay in shape so I would be ready to run again when the doctor cleared me. When I finally went out for my first run, I went only a mile. It took me twelve minutes, four minutes slower than my former pace and it wasn't pretty. My good leg wanted to run, but my bad leg felt like a wooden stump. I imagine my form looked like a step hop, but I was out on the trail. This was what my soul needed, no matter how awkward it was. I heard the voice telling me again; I would not run like this forever. I kept training and that fall I placed fifth for my age group in a 5K; my average mile pace was nine minutes and twenty nine seconds. By then I had lost the limp. It has been seven years and I still run, and the small voice is always there encouraging me no matter what comes my way.

I'M NOT DYING
By Kerri Davidson

My only picture of my grandpa shows him on our teddy bear brown couch holding me on his lap in my favorite red-checked Strawberry Shortcake dress. I was so shy I'd hide behind the couch when babysitters came, but in this yellowed photo, I smiled in the safety of his gray cardigan sleeves.

Soon after the picture was taken, both grandpa and I got sick. I had a passing childhood illness and got better. Grandpa didn't. His face is still etched in my memory, not the breathing visage in the picture, but his closed eyes at his wake. That is the face I'll never forget, the one I stared at when I rested my chin on the casket and peeked down at him. I thought he was asleep, until I slowly realized he would never wake up. I cried hysterically for him and for me and for endings, realizing what death was before I was old enough to read the word.

The next week in my Wednesday night Bible class, the teacher began a multi-week lesson on Heaven—where you go when you die, where my grandpa was. She described golden paths and shiny gates and loving a Being I'd never met. She asked the class to draw Heaven's landscape as we imagined it, on paper with waxy crayons labeled Bittersweet, Burnt Sienna, and Flesh. I mixed the colors trying to create an atmosphere to call paradise, but there was no place I could draw that didn't scare me, no place I wanted to be but across the street in my home with my family. I was just beginning to learn about the world I lived in, I wasn't ready to picture a better place.

Every night after Bible class I was terrified to go to sleep—convinced that if I closed my eyes like grandpa, I would die too. After my mom tucked me in and turned out the light, I poked my head out of the covers and kept my eyes open so death couldn't sneak up on me. The street light from the church parking lot across the street made my room glow a soft yellow and I'd sit up in bed and peek at the church—its walls collaged with our visions of Heaven. My mom had told me I was

97

too young to die, that I was not sick like grandpa, but I couldn't risk believing her. I started to cry, crying loudly until my parents yelled across the hall, "Go to sleep! We have to work tomorrow, go to bed!" But I couldn't be frightened into sleep—I was too frightened of it already.

Eventually, my older sister started sneaking into my room. She'd kneel next to my bed, hold my chubby hand and tell me I was going to be okay. She'd dry my tears and sing me a song she made up on the spot. I'd watch her lips move as the melodies dropped my guard and lulled me to sleep in spite of myself. She did this every night, every week. I never stopped fearing death—does anyone really? But I did stop fearing sleep. Her song was my security.

It was my grandpa who taught me about death, but my sister taught me about life. I learned you cannot keep a constant vigil for some inevitable event, that you are going to be scared in life. But if you're lucky, you will have a hand to hold and a voice to sing you through the dark.

BABY STEPS
By Aphrodite Matsakis

I accept hope
In matters large and small
For without hope
Why live at all?
I can't forestall
My hopes and dreams
For the love I need
Because all I can see
Are the problems in my way
Some dreams may never be and
I might never get all I think
Is owed to me
But if one dream dies
I'll fly to the next
Lest I be bereft
Of everything I ever wanted
If all I do today
Is take few baby steps
That's okay
Those baby steps may lead nowhere
To a dream that will vanish in the air
Or that was never there
To be had in the first place
But if I'm to be true to me
I have to make a date
With destiny
Like many a blind date
My dream may not even show up
And I'll drink once more
From the cup of frustration and defeat

But I can't let it beat me down
To the ground
To a premature death
Of spirit and soul
Today I'll act
As if I'm twenty years old
And hope to find a treasure or two
Large or small
It doesn't matter at all
Just a nugget or two
Of feeling alive
Of feeling fulfilled and satisfied
Will do
Will keep me from being so blue
I trust I can help it happen today
If I but take the time to pray, pray, pray
And wait for God to show me the way

HE UNDERSTANDS
By Michele Lee Woodard

In rain soaked clothing there I stood.
Seeking for answers that weren't meant to be understood.
Where to go? Where to hide?
All I knew, I was dying inside.
Feeling let down from family and friends.
It seemed so simple.
WHY COULDN'T THEY UNDERSTAND?
My heart, it was hurting.
The pain, it wouldn't subside.
The tears, oh the tears I've cried.
I called out to God, but He seemed so far away.
Out of touch. Out of reach.
How long could this possibly stay?
One day at a time. I would whisper to myself.
You can make it! You can make it!
My silent plea for help!
Each new day brought a brand new task.
Facing the world.
Wishing it was my last.
But inside I continued to fight.
For my husband, my children, for my life.
I didn't give in, though I wanted so bad.
God could deliver me! I knew this in my head.
On my knees I would spend hours in prayer.
Until I had enough Faith through God's Grace and Power.
Weakened in flesh, I felt the burden of pain.
Delivered through sacrifice, a new journey began!
My strength was restored, my courage renewed.

The piercing scars were no longer scattered nor torn.
Freedom from all that dwelled within,
now dwells with my Father, my Savior, my Friend.
Praise to thee I thankfully give!
To the One who took my hand.
To the one who Understands!

EMPTY PRAYERS
By Judy Kirk

When a good friend dies
we lose a part of our soul
for we are who we love.
We rejoice for the privilege
of their friendship and grieve
for the part of us that died.

Their spirit helped ours soar
their laughter echoed our joy
their tears washed ours away.
Our thoughts are lost.
Victories will seem shallow,
prayers empty without their name
following in a certain progression.

Our challenge is accepting a sunrise
that doesn't include them in our day
and learning to say Amens
knowing the vigil is over.
We want to pull a blanket over our heads
curl up inside ourselves and listen to the quiet.
But we hear them shouting, "Live!"
and know we must get up.

A SINCERE LETTER OF GRATITUDE
By Carolyn Johnson

Dear Britt,

I never thought I would actually arrive at a place in my life where I would want to thank you, however, my gratitude is indeed way over due. Believe it or not, John encouraged me to write you this letter. I'm sure you are wondering "Who's John?" but I will get to him in a minute.

I want to start with you. When we married, I loved you with all my heart. I wanted to be your devoted wife, your confidante, your comfort zone. I wanted us to ride off in the sunset together, but alas, that was not to be.

You forced me to finally look inward, to dissect and digest what I really needed in a mate. The red flags of sarcasm, alcoholism, infidelity and eventual cruelty were always there, but I chose to ignore them. With me as your wife, I knew I could make you the man you should have always been, the man I knew you were capable of being, the man who would love me forever. But, as we both now know, my valiant efforts were in vain. I could not save you from yourself. Perhaps that was why you picked me? Perhaps that was why you wanted to kill me? Perhaps that's why you never really could?

You forced me from my hometown, but, as in fairy tales, my happily-ever-after ending did come true. You always kidded me about looking at the world through rose-colored glasses, but it has served me well. I relocated to the city I grew up hating, yet fell in love with in the end. I made new friends, who liked me for exactly who I was. I finally found my home, my center of gravity, my faith again. I knew it within one month of moving. I would never have ventured from my hometown without your influence.

I would not have voluntarily chosen to leave my support system, my group of friends and my family and my church. What surprised me were the new friends I made, albeit not life-long friends, were exactly like the friends I had at home, only older and wiser. Or maybe it was me who was older and wiser, but nonetheless, I was grateful you gave me the shove.

You forced me to face the sudden illness and untimely death of my father alone. I flew home, staring out the window of the airplane, a black dress in my carry bag, knowing I had to say goodbye to the one man who had always loved me, but it made me stronger. I knew I could handle whatever life had to offer.

You forced me back into the workforce as well, back into the career I had when I first met you. I was stunned to be welcomed into the fold with open arms, respected for my level of knowledge, experience and enthusiasm. Working again gave me back my confidence, my sense of importance. I never knew how much I had missed it.

And last but definitely not least, I wanted to thank you for liberating me from being your Mrs. You freed me to find a man, a mate, a lover, a friend who sings my heart song. Yes, it is John of whom I speak. He doesn't look like the man I would have dreamed of, but he puts me first, loves me unconditionally and is thrilled, even after almost seven years now, to call me his wife. Would you believe we married on the third anniversary of my father's death? John turned my sad tears to happy tears.

Without you, without the life we endured together, without being forced through the painful stages of grief, I would have never known what it felt like to be truly cherished by a husband and for that, I thank you from the bottom of my heart.

Here's to sunsets,
Carolyn

SOMEONE CRIES AND SOMEONE KNOCKS
By Sande Cropsey

Someone cries and Someone knocks
On a door that's always locked.
Please comfort me and keep me near,
Charge my faith not to fear,
Change me for all the world to see,
Leave no trace of what used to be.

Someone cries and Someone knocks
On a door that's always locked.
Please grant these humble prayers, I pray,
Dismiss me not another day.
Give me the strength to let you in,
Believe in you I have a friend.

Someone cries and Someone knocks
On a door that's always locked.
Increase my courage by two-fold
Help me to feel that love untold.
Give me the will to carry on
In a world where I don't belong.

Someone cries and Someone knocks,
Someone cries and Someone knocks. . . .
Be my bridge to a better place,
Flood my life and grant me grace,
Help me open the door today,
Be my Light, and light my way.
Someone prays and Someone knocks
Someone prays, Someone knocks,
On a door that is un-locked.

THE LAST SHOT
By Mindy Aber Barad

"God...who examines innermost thoughts and feelings...(literally:
kidneys and the heart)"
Jeremiah 11:20

"Don't worry," is Dina's personal refrain.

She must keep reminding herself, religiously, three times a day
(sometimes more!). Otherwise she'll worry with fervor.

Her husband Joseph has been challenged with disabilities such
as low iron in his blood and a kidney transplant, for several years. Most
recently his left leg was amputated above the knee due to a blood clot.

Joe's fever went up two days before the New Year. He hadn't
taken his required bi-weekly shot of Erythropoietin, to boost his
hemoglobin, for several days because he only had one left. Replenishing
the stock required quite a bit of planning and ordering in advance and
general juggling of their medical insurance, as well as pushing the
pharmacy to expedite the order.

Dina took Joe's temperature, and with only mild anxiety, she
called and left messages for several of his doctors: the transplant
nephrologist, the hematologist and their family doctor. After that, she
gave her husband a fever reducer, and sat down beside him on the
couch. She tried to remain calm and optimistic, and held his hand.
Bored with sitting quietly, she looked around the room and wondered,
"What else can I do?"

Dina scanned the living room: Joe was slouched on the couch,
surrounded by his wheelchair, walker and a small table full of pill
bottles, a blood pressure machine and glucose meter. She was squeezed
in between the wheelchair and her tiny patch of the couch. Her eyes
settled on her Book of Psalms on a table in the corner. Her husband's
eyes were closed; he was motionless. He did not look well. She got up
to retrieve the book, sat back down; she took Joe's hand and began to

106

plead: "God, what else does my husband need? You know better than me. What else should I do?"

Dina finished one chapter and checked if there were any messages on the phone. Then she opened the book again. Though the words offered her heart peace and serenity, her mind wandered off to entertain troublesome thoughts.

What if, God forbid, I have to take my husband to the emergency room? How will we get there? By ambulance? Will the ambulance attendants be strong enough to lift him down the fifteen steps? Joe hated the wailing of the siren, the bumpy ride, lying on the gurney.

Their son Joshua had taken the car to Yeshiva and he wouldn't be back for a few days. Dina wrestled with the idea of disturbing him while he was learning, and didn't want to do that...not right before the New Year. Still, she wished she wasn't so alone with the decision of what to do with Joseph.

The New Year! she thought. How could I forget? She quickly opened to Psalm 27, and thirstily read the verse: "God is my light! "Hashem Ori..."

"Don't worry," she reminded herself, "Hashem will raise up my head! Hashem will gather me in..."

Gratefully, she continued to recite Psalms – assured that everything would work out for the best.

"I really don't feel well," her husband said.

He opened his eyes. How long had she been enveloped by the Holy words? She had no idea, but the clock said one hour had passed.

"Why don't you take the last shot of Eryth (the shot even had a nickname)? You'll feel better."

"No, we should save it; it's the last one. The medication is on order, but who knows when it'll be available. If I take the last dose we'll be left with nothing. I don't want to risk that."

Dina could hear the anxiety in her husband's voice. He was clearly worried, but not taking the shot presented its own risk. She took Joe's blood pressure, securing the cuff around his arm. It was an arm that could once lift the heaviest Torah scroll high above the heads of the men in synagogue. Today she had to lift and position her husband's weakened arm. Dina squeezed the rubber bulb and the cuff expanded. Joe didn't even complain. His blood pressure was border-line to low. Dina didn't say anything. She glanced around the living room, hoping to see something else that would contribute a ray of positivity.

There! Right on the special New Year bookshelf! Next to the prayer books was The Book of Our Heritage – a well-worn soft covered copy by Rabbi Kitov. Why hadn't she spied that shelf earlier? The Vidui book for confession on Yom Kippur, with the English and Hebrew explanations – that was there, as well as Hilchot Teshuva, Maimonides' Laws of Repentance, with commentaries.

Dina silently thanked Rabbi Kitov as she read, "…from ancient times these have been days of reconciliation between Hashem and Israel…" She closed her eyes and held the book close in her hands. Reconciliation: the Jews were commemorating the forty days and nights that Moses was on Mount Sinai, coming closer and closer to Hashem, receiving the Torah directly from Him.

"We too are coming closer to Hashem, and He to us," Dina thought.

The clock ticked another hour away. Finally she put in a book mark on the page just after the paragraph that said that the 25th of the Jewish month of Elul was the day that the world was created. She tried to give her husband a drink, but he refused to eat or drink anything.

"Today is the 28th, the anniversary of the third day of creation," Dina thought. The day the Torah says is "'twice good' – pa'amayim ki-tov!"

She returned to King David's uplifting words, wondering if, then strengthening her resolve – hoping, praying for her husband to recover before the New Year, Rosh Hashana.

"You have to have the shot, even if it's the last one," Dina insisted again. "Remember that children's story? 'Something From Nothing'? Where the grandfather told the grandchildren not to worry? 'Hashem will provide…'? God always provides."

Joe didn't have the strength to argue, though it was obvious to Dina that he didn't want to comply.

Suddenly, the door opened and in walked their son Josh!

"What are you doing here?" Dina began. "How…how did you know we needed you…right now?" she asked incredulously.

Dina stopped herself short of throwing her arms around her nineteen-year-old son. "I was going to call you," she said, "but …um…we didn't want to disturb you."

"I just had a feeling," Josh shrugged, "I wanted a blessing from Dad before Rosh Hashanah," he tried to explain.

Some feeling, Dina thought. She knew that his 'feeling' had to have begun at least 45 minutes earlier, the travel distance between his Yeshiva and their home, while she had been deep in prayer.

Joseph opened his eyes, and Dina could see that her husband felt better just being in the presence of their eldest son.

"You see Joe, if Joshy came home without us even calling him, then surely I can give you the last shot and trust that the new medicine will be here soon, God willing."

Josh joined in encouraging his father to take the chance. Dina felt enormous relief when she gave her husband that precious shot. It made her realize how much she had been beside herself with worry!

Within less than thirty minutes, Joe began to feel better. He was able to sit up and bless their son, with noticeable concentration. "May God bless you, like Menashe and Ephraim..." There were tears in everyone's eyes.

Then the phone rang; it was the pharmacy. The back order, two weeks late, had just come in. The shots were available now. Thank God! Josh could drive to the pharmacy to get the medication.

The concept of 'reconciliation' resonates during the month of Elul, before the Jewish New Year. It is a challenging time, as we overhaul our lives, clean the deepest recesses. We must make the extra effort, while keeping in mind that as we reach out to Hashem, He approaches us.

God truly does examine "the kidneys and heart." So, we should try not to worry, trust that His dosage – and timing - are for the best.

IN YOUR HOUR OF DARKNESS
By Julia Katz

In your hour of darkness I may not be there
But we'll be reunited when the tide has turned
If you're broken-hearted you must dry your tears
Know though I may go, in time I will return
Do not feel discouraged while I'm away
Thinking you're forsaken and all alone
You must find your courage drawing from your faith
That someday I will come and take you home
I did not betray you when I disappeared
And I only pray you stay the way you are
I love you and if you listen you will hear
These words are written inside your heart
So while I will miss you and while I will grieve
Still I insist that you continue on
Even in the darkness, so long as you believe
I'm always with you for we are one

RUNNING FOR MALAIKA
by Maria Bruce, with Brandon Barr

I was just a shy, eight-year-old girl when I sprang onto my parent's bed and informed them that when I grew up, I was going to Africa to be a missionary doctor.

It was a simple — even ignorant — desire.

I can't remember who lit the spark, maybe some missionaries passing through our church. Whoever it was, that little spark quickly became a raging fire. As a teenager, my longing for Africa only intensified. With each passing year, my dream drew a little closer to reality. By the time I graduated high school, a trip was in the works. Somehow I had survived those seven hellish years from sixth to twelfth grade with all the pressures of that microcosmic world tugging at me. It was a miracle I could only credit to the grace of God.

When I turned eighteen, I made my first trip to Africa, where I spent nine months at a Kenyan orphanage. It was called the Ushindi Children's Home. From day one I fell in love with the brick and mortar buildings, and the beautiful children who lived there. Over the nine months I formed an inseparable friendship with one of the older African girls. She was a 13-year-old orphan named Amani. She had the most beautiful, bright-hearted spirit that flowed from her shining eyes and humungous smile. She called me Auntie. I guess she felt I was her family. Her parents had died of AIDS, and she was alone in the world. How so much light and peace could emerge from such terrible darkness is a miracle. Amani is one of those souls you remember for the rest of your life: when you think of them, you feel close to God.

The months flew by like days. Before I knew it, I was flying back home to California. Going back to the states was one of the most agonizing experiences of my life. Sure, I missed my family and friends, but I belonged in Africa. Before my plane had even landed, I was plotting out my next trip back. The following year I returned to Africa, stopping at orphanages in Tanzania and Malawi, before returning to

Amani and the Ushindi Children's Home. However, when I arrived at the Ushindi home, my heart was troubled. I'd picked up a burden from the orphanage in Malawi; a little four-year-old girl named Malaika.

My first day of administering first aid in Malawi, I spotted her in a line of children who came for medical care. I had no official training, but I did what I could for them, swabbing away dirt and grime from boils and infections. When little Malaika came up in line, my heart immediately went out to her. She had deep, open wounds on her feet and legs. One wound in particular was grotesquely large, and it was packed solid with dirt. Gently I washed her legs, but the grime in that one deep gash wouldn't come out.

I called over Kristie, the director of the Malawi orphanage, and we decided to take Malaika to a nearby clinic. The nurse cleaned out the wound and gave her an antibiotic. The entire time Malaika was strangely withdrawn. I sensed a looming sadness hanging over her. No smiles, no feelings at all. I went to bed that night, my thoughts consumed with her. To see a living, breathing child so emotionally dead; it is impossible to leave with your memory unscarred.

Later that week we had a church service at the home I was staying at, and some of the orphans came. I spotted Malaika standing alone. Her eyes were distant, and that same sadness hung on her face. When I called her over, her movements were sluggish, as if each step was without motivation or purpose. Any other orphan would have come running with a smile on their face, but not Malaika.

When she came, I placed her on my lap. Malaika was big for a four-year-old and after a while my legs began to tingle and ache under her weight. But I didn't dare move her. I thought to myself, "Maria, this is worth it – just to love her." So I held her there, and tried not to think about the throbbing.

As she sat there, I noticed an awful smell coming from her. Having worked in Africa, where the closest thing to a shower is rinsing your arms and legs in water, I knew all about bad smells, but this was horribly different. It was almost unbearable. Immediately an old conversation sprang to mind that I'd had with my good friend Gentry who worked at the Ushindi Children's Home. A girl with a terrible smell had passed through their orphanage. One of the teachers had caught the stench coming off her and knew something was wrong, and it was later discovered that the girl was being raped.

Holding Malaika, I couldn't help worry about her stench. Did it mean anything?

For the next few days, I took her with me wherever I went. I would carry her around, as heavy as she was, and I would smile at her, and try to play with her. Even after all that, her face was cold. She didn't talk, and she wouldn't smile. Emotionally she was a corpse.

112

Seeing her like that, unable to experience any form of happiness, tore me up inside. I felt what Malaika needed was continual love, so I attempted to have her stay with me. You see, the Malawi orphanage was a single school building, and most of the orphans went their own way at night. I didn't know where Malaika went, and since she didn't talk, I had to ask around. I discovered that Malaika lived with her grandmother, a woman known for her cruelty. Repeatedly I was told that her grandma wouldn't approve of her staying with me. Uneasy about pressing the matter, I let it go.

The night before I was to leave Malawi for the Ushindi Children's Home in Kenya, a small miracle happened. Malaika was allowed to stay the night with me. A second miracle soon followed. Struck by inspiration, I reached out and tickled her. Suddenly her face broke out into a smile, and then gushing from her lips came an angelic laughter! I was so overwhelmed, I started shaking. It was beautiful, the transformation on that little face. I just kept tickling her. I didn't dare stop. Whatever trauma had rendered Malaika's heart so calloused was being undone before my eyes!

That night as she lay asleep beside me, I again began to worry for her. She was safe now, but in the morning I would be leaving. She still had that smell, and that nagging fear inside me wouldn't go away. Was she being sexually abused?

In the morning I revealed my fears to Kristie. When the jeep came to take me to the airport, Kristie and Malaika came along, and the driver dropped them off at the clinic for a physical check-up. It was hard leaving for Kenya without knowing. All I could do was hope that my fears were in vain.

That first morning at the Ushindi Children's Home in Kenya, I awoke to the sound of children singing. I forced myself out of bed. It was 5 a.m., and the children were having their Saturday morning praise and prayer service. Immediately I was filled with worry for Malaika.

I made my way out into the morning darkness. In the distance I could hear the beautiful orphan voices lifting praise to God. I'd spent nine months with these children the year before, and every Saturday morning they woke, of their own accord, and met before the sun rose to worship. Imagine, a room full of orphans crying out to God, the Father to the fatherless. His Presence was heavy in that place.

I found a spot in the back and joined in their praises. One by one they came over and hugged me as they continued to sing. It was moving, seeing all those old faces, but overriding all the joy was my fear for Malaika. When it came time for prayer, I put in my request. As discreetly as possible, I asked the children to pray for a little girl in Malawi, simply telling them that I feared she was being abused.

It was later that morning I received the phone call from Kristie, and her message broke my heart. "Your suspicions were right," she said, "Malaika has been raped."

The worst part was, I knew there was nothing I or Kristie could do about it. Justice is not a word one associates with Africa, and in Malawi, one has to catch a person in the act of rape for the police to intervene.

I felt weak and helpless. Would Malaika be just another statistic — just another faceless child -- devoured by evil men?

That night I was working in the kitchen making Mandazi (fried African bread), when Amani poked her head inside and asked if she could help. I was delighted to have the company. We talked for a while about the orphanage, and some of the changes it had undergone since I left. I sensed an unusual heaviness in Amani's voice. She didn't seem herself. A few seconds of silence passed, and then she said: "Auntie...was Malaika raped?"

Amani's directness caught me off guard. "Yes," I told her.

"Oh — oh," came Amani's pained response. Her countenance fell, and tears began to pour down her face. "How could someone do this?"

I shook my head, unsure how to respond.

She looked at me, her eyes searching, "Why didn't you bring her with you?"

The question left me breathless as I followed her simple logic. My heart was pierced. "It's illegal," I finally said, grasping at reason. "I wanted to."

"Auntie Maria," she said, "you could have just run with her."

"Amani, I could get in serious trouble."

She looked up at me, her face in anguish. "If I was there, I would have taken that girl and run."

I couldn't fathom where her deep compassion came from. She didn't even know this little girl, but here she was, ready to risk her life for her. The worst thing of all, deep inside me, I knew she was right.

"Maria," she finally said, "when I'm older, and my schooling is done, I will save those girls. I'm going to run with little girls like Malaika!"

That night as I lay in bed I buried my face in my arm. "God," I prayed silently, "you gave me the desire to follow you to Africa; I beg you...give Amani the courage to run."

114

DINING WITH LAZARUS
By Robert B. Moreland

How often is there a second chance
when life has dealt the final blow?
Death sits at the threshold snarling,
an irate phantom of my fears.

What would it have been like to dine
with Lazarus; now fresh from the grave-
Mary and Martha setting the feast for
the man Christ raised from the dead?

The disease was as fatal as insidious,
consuming your essence from inside.
But as they give you a short time to live,
the cancer is gone, no longer there!

Today I stared specter in the eye,
he blinked as I got you back again.
Blessed miracle yes! Oh carpe diem!
Feast on the moments that remain.

I'LL MEET YOU THERE
By Olga Mancuso

Holding love in one hand
And magic in the other,
Hands to work, hearts to God,
The eternal love of Mother.

Those who want to sing
Will always find a song.
My child, heaven has in store,
What was but now is gone.

Light a candle and pray;
Feel your soul *renewed*.
You can do all things, my son,
In Christ, *who* strengthens *you*.

Whisper my name in your heart,
I'll meet you in *every* prayer;
I've returned to where we began, and
I'll meet you in *every* dream there!

Death's but a thorn in *roses*;
Be *glad* for each new day,
Silhouetted against the sky,
My sunflower; *my bouquet*.

Letting go, so bittersweet,
My love for you so tangible.
The essence of faith to dare,
Reunions unimaginable.

Go on confidently, dear son,
My life's love — a blooming flower.
Live happily in the *now*,
We'll meet at the appointed hour.

Look to God in your soul-searching;
The secret of life is to care.
Heart-healing, dream-weaving —
Every breath, I'll meet you there!

WHAT IS HOPE?
By Susan Willms Fast

I am a survivor of depression! The long road I have taken; from being the little church mouse who was afraid of her own shadow to the woman God wants me to be, has been long and bumpy.

Somewhere deep within, I knew things could and would get better. When and how was up to God. Is that what hope is?

"What was missing?" was the question I asked myself. I found the answer; I was leaving Christ out of the equation. Everything I tried on my own was not working.

My healing began when I chose to get back into the word of God, starting with the book of John in the New Testament of the Bible. From there, I started to go to church on a more regular basis. I had learned from the book of John, we, as Christians, need the companionship and nurturing from fellow Christians.

While going back to adult Sunday school and joining bible studies, I learned that Jesus still loves me and I still love Him, but the positive feelings were buried under a lot of negative thoughts and feelings. I realized I still had a lot of pent-up emotions roaming around my head. With our pastor's help, I started a support group, which we both felt would be beneficial to all who would join.

Guess what? No one showed up the first night. The pastor and I both knew there were people in our congregation who would benefit, but were just as afraid as I was to share my struggles. Needless to say, after a few phone calls, we had between 8 and 10 come out each night.

It was of great help to all of us, being together in a spirit-filled support group, sharing similar feelings and knowing that anonymity was spoken at our meetings. We all came to the realization: God does not give up on us, so why should we give up on ourselves?

Pride was also a big factor of which I had to let go. The pride I am talking about here is about not being able to humble myself before God and admit I could not get better without His help. Most of the time the "me syndrome" is a root of many of our ailments, such as wanting things to happen the way we think it should.

I found I have a glorious God, who does not give up on me. Each time I wanted to, He gave me a ray of sunshine, using and reminding me of the blessings He had sent my way. It always led me to hope that I would get better. The ups and downs were easier to take the more I relied on my Lord. Thank you Jesus.

The following verses spoke volumes about the word of God, *Romans 8:24-26 N.I.V.:*

> For in this hope we were saved.
> But hope that is seen is not Hope at all.
> Who hopes for what he already has?
> But we hope for what we do not yet have,
> we wait for it patiently. In the same way,
> the Spirit helps us in our weakness.

Glimmers of hope got me through the worst parts of my depression, but why was I not able to recognize this or feel it at all times? Was it fear, unhappiness, anxiety, anger, or just plain ignorance of what the word of God really had to offer? Possibly they all played a factor in my downfall.

Was I not Christian enough? I felt I was. Told people I was, insisted, in fact. What I found out down the line was, yes I was a believer in Christ, but not mature enough in my faith to know what God wanted of me. Nevertheless, that hope, that inevitable hope that things would get better, kept me going. Otherwise, why was I able to function properly at times?

Hope got me out of my agonizing stress and pulled me out of the depths of anxiety and panic attacks. Hope held my head above the water line. Hope kept me searching God's words for answers. Hope told me my light would shine again, if I focused on Christ. Hope eventually led me to rest in the peace of God.

But why did it take so long? Perhaps God needed to let me go through all my trials, so I would learn to love and rely on Him alone. That is what He wanted all along, but the enemy tried incessantly to blind the fact. However the enemy did not win! My hope and trust in God were too strong for him to get through. The more I relied on God, the less trouble I had and the better I coped as each day passed.

Even though the enemy still tries to put a damper on things, he cannot devastate me to the point of depression anymore; thanks to God's hope and trusting Him to get me through. Praise the Lord! Hope is trust - trust is living in hope for what God wants of all of us, to be a child of God and live more Christ-like. Hope that God's goal for us will be reached with assurance, before His return.

So how does hope really work? In my evaluation, it is in my striving to reach the God-given goals or tasks He assigns to me, as best I can. Thanking my Lord and Savior for being there for me when I ask Him for help to attain them.

Hope is not wishing for things or that people should help us. Hope does not mean that all is well with our world or life at all times. Hope is not without a lot of work on our part due to wrong choices we make. Hope is filled with blessings, when we let the Holy Spirit move within us as we pray for God's will to be done. Hope allows us to encourage, thereby nurturing each other. I hope that you will know and feel God's overwhelming love. I hope that you know the Lord. God does not exist for our pleasure, but we for His. Hope allows us to be free to serve God. We are to hope in His truths with our heart, soul, and mind. Hope in God's specialties - (impossibilities).

I am a Child of God, striving daily to be the person God wants me to be. It is not easy at times, but my faith and hope are helping me to keep my eyes on Jesus through a personal relationship with Him. I cannot thank Him enough without feeling sad that I am still letting Him down from time to time.

However, like the rest of you, our struggles will not be finished until we meet Jesus in Heaven. Sometimes I want to go now, but that is being very selfish, don't you think? Why? Because God still has a use for me. It is up to me to wait patiently in hope; that He will let me know when and where He wants me to help Him in His work.

TO SEE THE NIGHT SKY
By Lynn C. Johnston and Samuel Johnston

To see the night sky
Breathless beauty from afar
Clouds gently part the heavens
To reveal a twinkling star

By night, the star shines brightly
Giving hope to all who pray
And hang their hopes upon it
Tomorrow will bring a better day

But by morning light, the star is gone
Hidden by the pale blue sky
And all the hope of last night's dream
Valiantly struggles not to die

At last, the daylight fades
And the star boldly reappears
It twinkles as if saying
"I was always here"

Constant in the heavens
Stars remind me to believe
That dreams obscured by daylight
Need faith and time to be achieved

TALK TO GOD
By Vanessa A. Jackson Austin

When you feel abandoned and alone,
Talk to God,
For He will never lead you wrong.
When you think no one cares,
Talk to God,
For all your burdens He will bear.
When you are downward and feel discouraged,
Talk to God,
To give you His favor and His courage.
When you feel raggedy and worn,
Talk to God,
For His strength will carry you on.
When the road you are traveling seems too bumpy for you,
Just *Talk to God,*
For His mercy will help you make it through.

A JEW FINDS GRACE
by Nikki Rottenberg

"Barach a ta, adoni elohanu melach olam......."

The Rabbi's voice, like that of a skilled singer, clear and melodious echoed throughout the temple hall as he recited the Jewish prayers. His body swayed in rhythm back and forth. The women and girls sat quietly on the left side of the congregation, their heads covered with white handkerchiefs, following along in their prayer books. On the other side of the room, the men and young boys, dressed in black suits, their blue and white talus's (prayer cloth) draped over their heads and shoulders, stood together rocking back and forth in unison with the Rabbi. Their voices as one, responded intermittently at various intervals with prayers of acknowledgement and agreement.

I sat beside my mother and sister, gazing around the temple. My eyes rested on the Torah displayed on the front platform behind the Rabbi. The velvet curtains which were usually closed had been opened, revealing the holy scriptures for all to see. Looking at the Torah was considered a sin when not done in specific ways and at certain times. The mood that morning in the synagogue was sacred.

After the service, we walked home. It was forbidden to drive on the Sabbath. Before entering our house, we kissed the mazuzah, a small decorative case that held scriptures from the book of Deuteronomy. We attached these to every door in our home in compliance with the teaching to write God's commandments on the doorpost of our house.

Raised in a strict observant Jewish home, I learned from a young age, that in order to please God and earn His favor, I needed to adhere to a myriad of rules and obligations. We weren't allowed to drive the car, answer the phone or doorbell, watch television, listen to the radio or turn the lights on during the Sabbath and on certain holidays. An endless list of do's and don'ts centered around food and eating. We kept two sets of dishes, pots, pans and cutlery; one for meat products and one for milk.

123

The two food groups could not come into contact with each other. All meats had to be blessed by a Rabbi and deemed 'kosher' or clean before we could consume them and certain foods were strictly forbidden such as pork or shellfish.

In my mid twenties, I experienced a dramatic encounter with Christ. I came to understand the Messiah spoken about in the book of Isaiah chapter 53, referred to the death and resurrection of Jesus. Convinced He was the way of salvation and peace, I committed my life to serving Him. I began to study the scriptures. As I poured over the Word, I discovered my efforts to abide by the Law with all its rules and traditions could never have brought me close to God. As I studied, I realized the purpose of the Law served only to point me to my need of grace and mercy. It was simply impossible to maintain all the required rules the Old Testament laid out.

When I lived my life trying to follow the letter of the Law, I walked in spiritual darkness. I tried by my own efforts to please God, but as I continued to read the Bible, "the unfolding of the Word gave light and understanding" (*Psalms. 119:130*). I discovered true access to the Father could only come through grace. Accepting God's wonderful gift of salvation, I experienced a sense of freedom I had not felt before. The burden of trying to work my way into God's favor was replaced with a deep gratitude. His way of reconciliation between Him and man was given freely and not based on what I did or didn't do. All I had to do was accept God's provision, knowing that truth turned the light on for me. By grace I am saved. It is a gift of God.

LIVING TO THE FULL
By Barbara Mayer

I will not die an unlived life,
I will drink it to the brim,
with no limits or boundaries,
tasting both sweet and bitter,
embracing all with open heart.
I will breathe in the marvel and
redolence of lilies and lapis lazuli,
orioles and onions, each created thing.
I will bear the pain of death and loss,
defeat and suffering, knowing
that all greens my growth.

When darkness clouds my days
and lethargy impedes my spirit,
adjust my lenses, make me see
the sparkle, the glow, the splendor
of each leaf and petal and hue,
vibrating in the crannies of creation.
Let no friend's face, or bird's song
go unnoticed. Let me be aware
of raindrops on my skin, sand between
my toes, breezes caressing my body,
and give thanks for every breath I take.

THE BEGINNING OF THE ROAD
By Karimah bint Abdul-Aziz

For so many years, I floundered in the terrifying environment of spiritual darkness. I sought a God of my understanding, but all the maps I was given to aid me in my quest were flawed, or inaccurate, or just plain deceptive. For a time I gave up. I still believed that there was a God, but I thought that He didn't believe in me.

Eventually, active addiction brought me to the place where I had to make a crucial decision; to die or to ask for help and thereby choose life. I chose life, although at that point I was unsure of what that really meant. I entered a rehab program, then moved to a halfway house and completed an aftercare program. I got a sponsor and we began intensive step work.

Step One: *"Admit that we were powerless over alcohol, that our lives had become unmanageable."* That one was quite easy. The realization of my powerlessness over alcohol was what led to my life versus death decision. Somewhere along the line, I lost the control and the drinks began to control me. The resulting unmanageability was clearly evident to everyone, and finally even to me.

Step Two: *"Come to believe that a Power greater than ourselves could restore us to sanity."* Working on this step was extraordinarily painful. You have to face the insanity of your life in order to recognize your need for a restoration of sanity. To face myself, without self-medication, was the emotional equivalent of an appendectomy without anesthesia. I clung closely to my sponsor during this time because she was the Power greater than myself.

Time passed, and I completed my foray into the minefield of my past. Amazingly I experienced a new-found sense of freedom and of hope. I could dimly discern the outlines of a positive future, of a real life.

It was time to move on to Step Three: *"Make a decision to turn our will and our lives over to the care of God as we understood Him."* Uh oh, here comes trouble! I didn't understand God at all, and I was pretty

126

convinced that He didn't understand me either. I recognized my sponsor's power because I saw it working in my life on a daily basis. God, however, was a different story. I was operating with a borrowed God, but I was fairly certain that was not what step three meant.

I had moved out of the halfway house and into transitional housing. I made friends with another resident, and one evening he came to a meeting that I was chairing. Afterwards, we went out for coffee. He told me that he was a Muslim, "but not a 9/11 Muslim." (*This was October 2001, so he was understandably a bit paranoid.*) He was very dedicated to his faith, and talked a lot about it. I found what he said interesting, but I had learned from past experience not to accept what people told me at face value. So I decided to investigate for myself. In particular, I wanted to clarify the disparities between what he was saying and what the media was saying. I began my quest at the public library. I asked the librarian for assistance. Once she understood my search, she told me that I wouldn't find what I needed there. She advised me that I would be able to find an abundance of information at the Hartford Seminary, as they specialized in religious issues.

When I returned to the house, I asked one of the counselors about the seminary. He told me that the Duncan Black Macdonald Center for the Study of Islam and Christian/Muslim Relations was located there, and it had the oldest Christian/Muslim relations program in the US. He also told me that they had an extensive library which included a wealth of information about Islam. That was exactly what I needed. He gave me travel directions, and I went there the next day.

For the next week, I spent time almost every day at the seminary. I read and read, and I purchased a number of books for my personal library, including my first copy of the Holy Qur'an. It didn't take me long to recognize that my lifelong quest was over. I had found what I sought for so long. I had a God of my understanding.

Once I had a clear understanding of Islam, I was totally enthralled. I fell completely in love. What I loved most was having a one-on-one relationship with Allah. That was something that I had always craved and no one had ever been able to explain to me why this wasn't possible. But now I knew that it was.

I made my declaration of faith (shahada) on the first day of Ramadan that year: November 18, 2001. I have never once regretted that decision. On that day, I turned my will and my life over to the care of Allah, the God of my understanding. He has kept me clean and sober, even removing the desire to use from me. I have developed a strong sense of honor and integrity. I respect and love myself and am aware of my self-worth. I have self-confidence. I returned to school recently, to study Sociology and Psychology. I currently have a cumulative GPA of 3.97. I know that all these things are gifts and blessings from my God,

127

and I have a heart overflowing with gratitude. The life that I had been given brief tantalizing glimpses of early in recovery is clear and focused today. I am living it! The Twelve Steps and the religion of al-Islam form a protective barrier around my soul, keeping me safe from harm and affording me the freedom to continue to grow and change and flourish. I have received a wondrous healing; physical, mental, and spiritual. It is now my goal – no , it is my duty – to pass onto others what was so freely given to me. Today my life has meaning and purpose. I am free to be me; I am proud to be me. Being me has become a beautiful experience.

THE SEEING BLIND
By Melissa Kesead

My eyes have fluttered open
No longer one of the seeing blind
I'm running for the steep hill
Leaving reason far behind

My heart is beating faster
Not hindered by the pain
Of questions gone unanswered
My tears, they fall like rain

All my life I'm searching
Seeking for what's true
Looking for the answers
I've found them all in you

My ears are free from deafness
I finally hear the song
Of angels long forgotten
They've sung it for so long

My eyes have fluttered open
The mist before them cleared
I'm reaching for the unknown
And everything I've feared

All my life I'm searching
Seeking for what's true
Looking for the answers
I've found them all in you

HOPE
By Tanya Miller

"Hope is the thing with feathers—
That perches in the soul—
And sings the tune without the words—
And never stops—at all—
And sweetest—in the Gale—is heard—
And sore must be the storm—
That could abash the little Bird—
That kept so many warm—
I've heard it in the chilliest land—
And on the strangest Sea—
Yet—never—in Extremity—
It asked a crumb—of me."

(Emily Dickinson)

Emily Dickinson is right about most things, but dead wrong about hope.

"Today's the day," I say to Richard as I take the thermometer from my mouth. As I've been doing every morning for the past two years, I record my temperature first thing in the morning on the chart beside my bed. Today, it reads 98.2, a good five tenths of a degree higher than usual—the sign of an LH surge. I will now be fertile for about three days.

"Do we have to?" he groans. Even though we haven't had sex since this time last month, we both dread the night's activities. For him, the pressure is on. Big time. If things don't work right, we'll have to wait another whole month. An eternity. For me, it's just the start of an inevitable roller coaster ride on a thing called hope.

"Try not to act so excited," I say, as I shove out of bed and head for the bathroom to get ready for work.

130

"Maybe we should just take a month off," he calls from the bedroom.

"Are you kidding? And waste another thirty days? If I have to wait another minute more, I'll go crazy!"

"This thing is making you crazy. Let's just take a break and see what happens."

He's right about it making me crazy, although taking a break will not help, since the endless waiting is what's driving me crazy. Already, I am looking at the calendar, mentally circling April 26, two weeks from today. Already, I am swallowing my folic acid capsule and pouring myself the last cup of coffee I will allow myself that month. Already, I am telling myself that this month I will not get my hopes up.

But that's impossible. Every time I refuse a cup of coffee or a drink, I hope. Every time I take a prenatal vitamin (just in case), I hope. Every time I look at the calendar, I hope. It's impossible not to.

April 26. Every trip to the bathroom brings a mixture of anticipation and dread. I don't want to look down, but I force myself. Nothing. All day. But, I tell myself at the end of the day, it's only one day. Don't get your hopes up.

April 27, 28, 29, 30 – the same ritual every day for five days. Still I tell myself not to hope. After work, I stop at a little-used drug store, where I glance around to make sure no one I know is in the store before slipping the pregnancy test into my basket, along with toothpaste, hairspray, and Tylenol. The last thing I need is a small-town rumor.

It is impossible to buy a pregnancy test without hope. It is more impossible to perform the test without hope. I hold the stick in a dribble of urine and set it on the bathroom sink to wait. I can't just sit there and watch to see if there will be one line or two, so I mop the kitchen and bathroom floor. That way I will have to stay out of the bathroom until the floor is dry. No point in having my hopes dashed for nothing. Finally, the floor is dry, and I have no other excuse to keep me from looking. I steel myself against hope. "You know it's going to be negative," I tell myself. "It always is. So don't be disappointed."

One line.

I don't cry. I never do. But all the life drains out of me and spreads like a puddle on the bathroom floor.

Maybe it was wrong? How accurate can those things be, anyway? So I console myself – after all, no period yet. I'll just wait. May 1, 2, 3, 4, 5. So I continue to face the dreaded trips to the bathroom, and still no sign. Every time I leave the bathroom, I smile a little more and laugh a little more freely. That's it! The test was wrong! I'm not going to buy another one. I'll just wait until I am absolutely sure, and then I'll go to the doctor. May 6, 7. I've never been this late before!

May 8. Hope stabs me again, and I bleed.

I pour myself a stiff drink and curl up in the fetal position on the couch, my body split in two by menstrual cramps, my spirit split in two by disappointment.

When Richard comes home, I am still there.

"I'm not pregnant."

He puts up the foot rest of his recliner and looks at me with surprised confusion—why am I announcing such an obvious fact? Clearly, he has not been plagued by the hope that I have. But then again, he's not the one who had to look for the signs. "No, I'm not surprised. Why, did you think you were?"

"Well, I had hoped."

Cruelly, by the next LH surge, about two weeks later, hope will have made itself small again, but will already be starting to grow. A weed that will not die.

Hope is a thing with thistles—
That overruns the field—
And laughs at pesticides and hoes—
And never dies—at all—

And prickles—through the gloves—are felt—
And sore must be the hands—
That try to yank Hope up to save
The life robbed from the land.

Its roots grow deep into the earth—
I dig and dig some more—
Yet even when I think it's killed—
It's stronger than before.

AND I WILL GO THERE WITH YOU
For A.A .and M.A.
By Ysabel de la Rosa

Hay más tiempo que vida –
but time robbed you anyway, wresting your son
from this life – and yours
And now you feel a dagger in your heart
that killing edge which should have ended
all pulsing, but – *maldito sea* – your heart beats on

You know the sorrow that burns so deep
it feels as though it melts the marrow of your bones
You move through each hour like molten lead –
slow, and – so – hard – to – stir

You disbelieve that clocks can still count time
that the earth still whirls through an infinite sky
that nothing else stops, even though his life
stopped – so sudden – and – too soon
You live in two worlds now: the one that ended
and the one that goes on everywhere else but
inside you

I know what's next: you'll let yourself down
into the dark and narrow well called faith
and go blind with believing that yes
the good still lives, and God remains
our Good, even though you now
have shocking proof to the contrary
And I will go there with you

We'll go into the dark well of faith, you and I
without those we never thought to lose —
your grown son gone, and my little one lost
We will be more alone and more
together than before, sorrow knitting us
into a course communion

No simple drink this, but blood
no simple food this, but broken bones
Now, more than ever, we know how sacred
is our gift — and how hard it is to ingest
even one crumb, to swallow even
one sip of our faith's inheritance. And yet
we will break this bread and drink this cup
will share the unbearable, as we
affirm the unknowable, and trust that
our God who united us with His Son
will, in His own way, one day
unite us with our own.

RADIATION
By Gina Troisi

At Holy Family Hospital, white gowns surround me. Pink and blue diamond shapes decorate the gowns. My mother is waiting to be radiated. Two men sit across from us, side by side in johnnies and white socks. A younger gentleman accompanies one of the men—they murmur words back and forth. The other man in the johnny is by himself, reading *Time* magazine. Each Friday, in this waiting area, I prattle in my head, placing bets about what kinds of cancer invade the bodies underneath the gowns. My mother is allowed to wear pants with her garment. Platform shoes from Spain, with a wedged wooden heel and pink satin fabric, stick out from under her jeans.

The waiting room is the size of an office cubicle, and just as in a cube, snippets of life can be observed beyond the two walls dividing radiation waiting from the rest of the hospital. To the left are the lockers where the gowns are stored, and to the right, registration desks form a circle where nurses wheel patients in and out of rooms. My mother and I have intermittent conversations while I scribble notes, in hopes that they might gradually shape a story. We talk about her visit with a friend the day before, who has just flown in from New Mexico. How they went to Syms, their favorite bargain store, where they sometimes buy the same outfits since they live so far away from one another. My friend, Jen, and I do the same thing, I tell her. Even though we live close.

I say I made haddock smothered in crushed walnuts for dinner last night. I garnished the dish with our favorite Italian style greens with garlic and onion, broccoli and spinach. I say that I decided to chop up some green martini olives and throw them into the mix. Then, I added some capers. And some jalapenos.

She tells me that sounds delicious—that maybe I should try haddock piccata some time--it's just as easy as the chicken.

The technician peeks into the waiting room. She has long, jet black, shining hair. She calls one of the older men, the one who is alone. Before they walk away, my mother asks the technician what her kids dressed up as for Halloween. When the black-haired lady responds, my mother smiles wide at the answers, *witch* and *pumpkin*. "How cute," she says. She talks loud and cheerful. The technician leads the man away. He is hunched over, his eyes turned toward the thinning carpet.

An older, white haired woman wearing a nametag, which reads, *Mary, Chapel Intern* (I didn't know such a position existed), walks into the waiting room. She ignores the younger man across from us, and the woman sitting on the other side of my mother. "Hello," Mary says. "I'm from St. Joseph's Chapel and I was wondering if I could say a prayer for you both." She looks at my mother, in a gown over her denim, while I wear a black fleece shirt. *I know she wears a gown, but she is still too healthy for kneeling and praying. Isn't this a bit extreme?* My mother's complexion is hydrated and flawless, even pretty. She has full clusters of hair, which have been freshly curled. She smells like lilacs.

My mother is sitting in between a bald woman and myself. A white knitted cap hugs the bald woman's head. Her face is swollen. The two were just talking about how they both underwent surgery at the same hospital, Faulkner, in Boston. How my mother is completing her fourth week out of the six, and how the woman has just started here.

How does Mary know we are not a threesome? Surely, the bald woman looks sickly. *Why does Mary approach my mother first?*

My mother looks up at Mary. "Sure," she says. I look down at the purple carpeting. Mary stands in front of our seats and grabs each of our hands.

"And your name is?" Mary asks.

"Rose," my mother answers.

"And you are her?" Mary turns her head toward mine.

"Daughter," my mother says.

I hold Mary's hand loosely, and look straight ahead at the man across from me. He looks about fifteen years my senior. Maybe forty-five. The man with the bare legs, the one who hasn't been called in yet, is his father. *Prostate cancer*, I think. Mary starts talking aloud to God, mentioning something about His promises. She is bowing her head toward us, smiling. I'm expecting her to close her eyes, but she doesn't.

While Mary speaks, I am thinking about how hokey this is. *What does she do, roam the hospital looking for the patients who are the most likely to die?* I know that Mary must mean well, but while she speaks, I doubt the notion behind the enormous, male God, perched on a cloud. What promises is she speaking of?

I remember my CCD teacher saying, "Even bad thoughts count as sins. Even if you don't say something bad aloud, everything you

136

think can most certainly be counted as a sin. This is why you must go to confession." Remembering her statements provokes me to feel guilty about acts I don't even commit. *Did I mistakenly put anything sharp into the recycle bin before I put it outside on the street last night? Did I accidentally slit the wrists of a waste management worker?*

My mom has her eyes closed and I know she is squeezing Mary's hand because her veins are purple and thick and obtrusive. Here I am, having "bad thoughts" while Mary prays and my mother listens. I think the bad thoughts are even more tempting because they are forbidden, just as they were in the third grade, in the church classroom. The father and son are staring at us. My uneasiness grows. *When will this woman set my hand free?* It isn't that I'm uncomfortable with affection (although some people perceive me this way), but rather that Mary is going on about our mother-daughter love intensifying. My mother and I don't need breast cancer's invasion for our love to progress. We don't need to see death to know that we are important to one another.

We are already close; we have always been close.

The bald woman with the white cap is called in. The son and his father, with the prostate cancer, heed Mary. They are listening to her go on about sickness and health. I'm not sure if they are wishing she visits them next, or hoping she does not. Or, are they simply thinking about their own relationship? Their closeness?

In order to try to forget about cancer, I have been venturing down to the ocean with my notebook. But instead of forgetting, I write about cancer. It hangs over me like a black cloud that now circles my mother's world, like a planet revolving around the sun. I feel changed, as if my world has been tweaked, and there is no place inside of it that feels healing, or right. When my mother calls to ask how I am, I don't tell her that I feel as if I'm locked inside someone else's skin waiting to be let out. Instead, I say, "They caught it early. You'll be fine."

Mary finally let go. I clasp my hands. "Would you care for some Eucharist? I have some in my pocket," she says. I picture sweaty wafer chunks, lint speckled and sticking to the inside of Mary's pocket.

"No, no, thank you," my mother says. For a minute I thought she might say "yes," and start munching on the wafer while the others stare.

Mary is done with us now. She walks over to the man and his father.

My mother squeezes my knee. "I know you were uncomfortable with that," she says. "But, don't you think it was nice, what she was saying about our relationship?"

"Yeah, and it gave me a story idea," I say.

"Oh Gina, she's just doing her job. She doesn't even get paid. She's just a good person trying to make people feel better and give them some hope."

I look at my mother's pleading eyes. "You're not going to die, you know," I whisper.

"I know," my mother nods and kisses me on the cheek.

The black haired lady approaches the cubicle, "Rose, you're up."

The woman with the white cap walks back in, but heads toward the lockers. On her way, she waves goodbye to us.

My mother stands up and drops her purse into my lap. The technician says, "I know it's Friday because you have your daughter with you."

"Yes," my mother says, smiling, ready to follow her. "Another week is almost behind me." Radiation is like a nine to five job; you get the weekends off.

I watch Mary bless the father and son, and look back at my notebook. My pen scratches the sentence: *You are not going to die*.

SAVING GROUND
By Nancy Brewka-Clark

The last race of the season is going off late.
The heavens have started to spit a cold rain,
staining the churned tan of rutted dirt to
tobacco brown. A few die-hard fans
dot the wide asphalt apron, but the three of us
cling to the rail by the trail where the horses,
riders up, will soon come ambling down.

Taped trumpet notes as familiar as "Taps"
spark a last charge to the betting windows.
My mother Annie, eighty-two, always goes for
odd-ball names like Henbane or Baldski.
Tom, my husband, combs *The Racing Form*.
I, facing surgery in a few days for a first-stage
malignancy of the right breast, scrutinize
the six-point type of dam and sire, trainer,
owner, markings on the jockey's silks,
looking for divine guidance
among these cheapest of fillies and mares
stabled at the bottom of luck's barrel.

I have always been prayerful, clandestinely so,
and never more so than now. My mother
has just paraded before Tom and me in
her kitchen, topless and one-breasted,
as withered and sallow as a store brand of
roasting chicken, seasoned and flecked
with Kerasotes and liver spots, in a reminder
that she has gone for more than thirty years
without a breast and without mentioning

the loss, even to her own sisters, so I can, too.
It's a double-edged sword, that message,
but I've decided to go her route and play
my cards close to the vest, reasoning that
I won't tell anyone unless I lose my hair
like my sister did from her chemo, after which
she recovered, turned fifty, and got married.

The clubhouse is lit up behind us like some kind
of grand cruise ship, giant glass walls reflecting
the watery scene, damp earth, slanting rain,
black sky, and the white-hot numbers flashing
the relentlessly fluctuating odds on the tote board.
"Muddler," I say. Annie grins. Tom frowns.
"Eleven to one, and good in the mud," I say.
But what I really mean is that I am muddled,
churned up, blaming myself for dying young
(or at least, at forty-seven, not that old)
if I do, which I fervently hope that I don't,
but might, thought I don't believe I will.

A bell shrills. Gates clang. "They're off!"
Running in pools of darkness, straining for home,
this handful of horses faces the end of the line,
either too slow or too unpredictable to have won
more than a single race in the past six months.
Muddler, small and brown, breaks fast,
but drops to last when her jockey is forced
to swing wide on the far outside.

"Run like the wind," I pray to her, invisible
as the breathing God riffling dark waters.

Muddler gallops into sight in the backstretch,
trailing the pack but edging up on the rail as
she senses there's a way of saving ground.
In the far turn, Muddler's number on the board
flashes to fourth, then third, then second. At the
sixteenth pole Muddler lunges forward, and wins.

Her faith in beating the odds will stay with me
under the wire, under the knife, under the gun,
through all the victory laps that I will run.

A MOUNTAIN TOP EXPERIENCE AND HOW IT CHANGED ME

By Karen Elvin

After working as a school counselor for four years, I felt the need for self renewal. In talking with a friend about stress management, she asked me if I had ever taken a retreat. I began to search for a place near where I lived. I discovered Frenchville, PA offered just what I was looking for.

Following a 45-minute drive through a mountain area, I soon found myself unpacking my suitcase. The room was simply decorated with a beige and brown patchwork quilt, a desk, dresser and one reading lamp.

The weekend offered not only solitude but a counseling session with a Catholic Sister. After explaining about some of the anxiety that I had been feeling in my demanding job, she asked me if I would enjoy painting about what I was experiencing. That would be just "my cup of tea."

Gathering up a few supplies in a tote bag, I began an outdoor hike up the Calavary Hill. At the top was a spectacular view of the surrounding hills of beautiful Clearfield, PA and a rustic wooden bench which faced a large rugged cross. I soon began sketching the landscape on my paper pad. I noticed dark clouds were gathering in the distance. For just a few moments, some bright sun rays broke through the lower clouds closer to me.

I began to reflect how the sun or "Son" is always there and present, even if I may not visibly see it. I wondered if that was going on in my life. The time soon passed, I packed away my sketch materials and started back down the hill.

I was beginning to sense an inner peace spreading through my body.

141

After this time of solitude, I returned home and enrolled in a nearby seminary school for some advanced classes. I had in mind some counseling-related experience in lay ministry.

After many family adjustments, we moved to western Pennsylvania and I had an opportunity to take a class in art therapy. Soon, I was combining art therapy with my work as a child and family therapist. What an adventure I had in many remote areas as my job was a mobile therapist. I learned that in spite of many traumas for children, the Holy Spirit was always present in each situation. Each child learned to express themselves in healthy manners through art.

My work has been documented in a DVD for a television special, called "The Creative Life." I was asked to exhibit my art work to honor all seniors who are living in a creative manner.

Lately, back and knee surgery has slowed my body along with arthritis and aging. Currently I teach my five-year-old granddaughter to paint and a class at nearby museum.

Not only do I enjoy beautiful scenes when I travel, but I've even painted breathtaking sunrises and sunsets from our new home near a wooded and creek walkway. God has been so gracious and good to me and my family.

I have felt His Mercy and Grace and try to express that in each of my paintings.

When dark clouds do appear in our daily experiences, I am reminded that God's love and goodness are just beyond.

The study of nature's beautiful landscapes has opened my eyes to God's goodness in everyday circumstances.

PETITION FOR PIETY
By Amy S. Pacini

When I was born
God breathed life into my soul
When I stumbled to the ground
God lifted me up in his arms
When I cried out in pain
God healed my wounds
When I surrendered myself to the world
God rescued me
When I asked for mercy
God offered me another chance
When I was cold
God offered me a blanket
When I was hungry
God gave me the bread of life
When I was thirsty
God poured his holy water upon me
When I became poor
God brought me wealth
When I lost my way
God served as my divine compass
When I was afraid
God gave me courage
When I was anxious
God washed his peace over me
When I was weak
God gave me almighty strength
When I felt alone
God walked beside me
When I needed love
God wrapped his heart around me

When I faced temptation
God offered me salvation
When I doubted myself
God believed in me
When I was overcome with despair
God gave me hope
When I was filled with shame
God cleansed me with his glory
When I was afflicted by misfortune
God delivered a multitude of blessings
When I was consumed with ignorance
God provided me with eternal wisdom
When I am wrong
God is always right
When I sin
God is always pure
When I trust him
God will provide for me
When I follow him
God will lead the way
To a better life
Than any I could have ever chosen.

DONNA DE LA PENA
By Hanoch Guy

You who have been worshipping all your life
in cathedrals, mighty mosques and grand synagogues
Go on a hejra to the lovely village of Mijhas in Spain
Go up the small hill
ignore the adorned donkeys
At the top of the hill you will find
the Madonna of Pena
is present in the tiny cave-church
Only few pews
a single wooden altar with a brass cup and a simple cross
She smiles and welcomes you to add your offering
to the side alcove
Braids of a young girl
henna colored hair of a new bride
a sliver of a war veteran crutch
a doll's foot
by a crippled boy
A button is the latest offering from a widow's black dress
who kisses the concrete floor
Merciful Donna will take your offering too
lit a small candle asking for healing
her hand on your forehead
Gentle and cool

One day the villagers decided to expand the church
and a fire broke out and burned four acres
around the church
The whole mountainside was charred
The fire stopped at the mouth of the cave
It spared the blooming oleander above
The townsfolk understood
Let the flame remain
within Donna de la Pena

Stand perfectly still
Close your eyes
Healing fire will bathe you
stay within you on the journey back

About the Contributors

Karimah bint Abdul-Aziz -- This will be my first time ever being published. Although I have always written, when I returned to school in the fall of 2008, my English professor encouraged me to write for others, not just myself. She felt that I had a real talent, and she had me enter an Arts and Sciences Division essay contest. I won the Kwame Ahooffe Memorial $1000 scholarship award. The following semester, my second term professor was a professional writer and it is she who encouraged me to start submitting my work. I write because I have so much to say. It is part of who I am.

Mindy Aber Barad moved to Israel in 1977. She has a BA from Washington University (St. Louis) and an LLB from Hebrew University. She practiced law, but writing is her first career choice. In 1997 she won second prize in the Jewish Librarians' Choice competition for a children's story. Her poetry, stories, book reviews and essays have been published in *Wild Plum, Current Accounts, the Jerusalem Post, the Jewish Press* and other publications both on and off line. Most recently Mindy has become the Israeli co-editor of *The Deronda Review*.

Kimberly Alfrey is a mother of three grown children. Over the years they have inspired many poems. She has written poetry for over 35 years and finds inspiration in the smallest of things sometimes. "Dream High" was inspired by her recent trip to Cades Cove in the Great Smokey Mountains.

Bernice Angoh is originally from Cameroon, West Africa. She won the Editor's Choice Award in 2003, 2005 and 2007 from the International

Library of Poetry. Her poems have been published in several anthologies and her articles grace pages of the renowned BHF Magazine, where she is a writer and contributing editor. Bernice has been nominated several times for the prestigious 'Poet of the Year' and her first book, *Lemonade Street,* a success, still enjoys rave reviews from readers worldwide. With all that said, nothing can put to words the highly anticipated publication of her second book, *When a Woman Loves a Man,* which will be released just in time for Christmas. You can read more about the author at www.berniceangoh.com or www.lemonadestreet.net. Bernice is also a wife, a mother, a photographer, a songwriter and founder of the Forever Young Revolution, a company she started because of her love for exercising and eating healthy.

Connie Arnold is an author and poet residing in Winston-Salem, North Carolina with her husband and has two children and three grandchildren. She is the author of *Beautiful Moments of Joy & Peace* and *Abiding Hope & Love,* inspirational poetry collections. Her writing has been published in *Forever Friends* Anthology, *Secret Place* Magazine, *PrayerWorks, Empowered Women Ezine,* Lupus Foundation of America's *Lupus Lifeline* newsletter and accepted for two more anthologies and a children's book. She posts new poems each week on her website, http://www.freewebs.com/conniearnold and blog, http://conniearnold.blogspot.com. Her poetry is uplifting and encouraging, helping those facing difficulties in life, as she does in living with lupus, finding hope and peace in the limitless love offered to each of us.

Vanessa A. Jackson Austin, who began writing poetry at a very young age, is the author of two books of poetry and quotes: *Refreshments for the Heart* and *Live On: Inspirational Poems and Quotes.* Her son, Cedric, and husband, Frederick, illustrated the covers of both books. She has been featured in *The Huntsville Times,* WAFF 48 News, WHAM-TV and several magazines. Born in Gadsden, Alabama, Vanessa is a stained glass and jewelry designer who owns CABBIT Designs in Harvest, Alabama. She is a member of the Alabama State Poetry Society, Alabama Writers; Forum, and Poets and Writers. She can be reached at cabbitdesigns@knology.net or via her websites: www.cabbitdesigns.net and www.cabbitdesigns.com.

Lucy Jane Barnett is a writer, artist, belly dancer and farmer who lives and works on a micro-farm in Eastern Ontario, Canada. Constantly exploring themes of divinity and whimsy, Lucy works to include spirituality in everything she grows or creates. While flummoxed in

148

writing her first story, she could not figure out how to spell George. Lucy now places rules of spelling aside and lets the words move through her. You can learn more at www.compostellae.com.

Brandon Barr is the co-author of the novel, *When the Sky Fell*. His short stories have appeared in *Residential Aliens, Haruah, Ray Gun Revival, Revelation Magazine, Digital Dragon*, among others. His newest novel, *Midnight over Midian*, is a story of church persecution, and the struggles of a young girl caught in a radically changing American culture. The novel is due out in 2010. Visit Brandon at www.brandonbarr.com

Glenda Barrett, a native of North Georgia is an artist, poet and writer. Her paintings are on an online gallery called Yessy.com, and at this time her first poetry chapbook titled, *"When the Sap Rises,"* is on display on Amazon.com. Glenda's work has been published in *Woman's World, Journal of Kentucky Studies, Chicken Soup for the Soul, Farm & Ranch Living, Rural Heritage, Psychology for Living, Smoky Mountain Living, Georgia Magazine, Living with Loss Magazine* and many others.

Susan Berg is a freelance marketing communications consultant with a professional background as a Communications Manager in the Chamber of Commerce industry where she produced award-winning Chamber newsletters and marketing materials. Her background also includes working as an auto sports reporter several years ago, covering the racing events for the *USAC Western States Midgets & TQ Series* with articles published in *National Speed Sport News, Western Racing News* and *Racing Wheels*. Susan lives in Southern California with her family where she enjoys oil painting and is currently working on her first children's book, which she hopes will soon be published in order to fulfill her life-long dream of being a published author. For more information, Susan can be reached via email at ice.bergs@yahoo.com.

Sandra Berris was co-founder of *Whetstone* in 1982, which she edited until 2000. The Literary Magazine garnered numerous Illinois Arts Council/NEA annual literary awards and a 1995 American Literary Magazine Award for editorial excellence. Her poems have appeared in many little magazines including *Arts Alive, The Midwest Quarterly, Prairie Schooner, Rhino* and *Willow Review*. She was a recipient of Prairie Schooner's Hugh J Luke Poetry Prize, and her poem *Clock Shoe* was included in the anthology *Best of Prairie Schooner* (University of Nebraska Press, 2001).

Francine L. Billingslea – I am a mother, grandmother, a breast cancer survivor and a newlywed for the second time around. I have recently

149

found a passion for writing and have been published in several anthologies, including *Chicken Soup For the Soul: Divorce and Recovery, Memories of Mother, Motherwise II, Liberated Muse, How I Freed My Soul Book I, The Rambler Magazine* and online for *Guideposts*. I love writing, traveling and spending quality time with my loved ones. My inspirational memoir, *Through It All* will be available early fall of 2009.

Marguerite Guzmán Bouvard is the author of 6 books of poetry, her latest *The Unpredictability of Light* was published this year. She has also written 11 non-fiction books in the fields of human rights, grief, illness and women's issues and numerous articles on illness and spirituality. She is a Resident Scholar at the Center for Research on Women, Brandeis University.

Maria Bruce is a native of California. Since meeting Malaika and caring for her physical needs, Maria has been pursuing a bachelor's degree in science and begins nursing school fall 2009. With these new skills, her desire is to return to Africa and continue to love and care for the needs of children like Malaika. The burden still weighs heavy on her.

While **Nancy Brewka-Clark** is a produced playwright, published poet and longtime writer of short fiction, her first job was in newspapers and it was there that she learned to distinguish fact from fiction only to mix them up with joyous results. She lives on Boston's North Shore with her husband Tom, a fellow writer and her beloved sounding board.

Gwendolyn Carr – Although my writing career began when I was over fifty, I have published three poetry books: *Starts and Songs, Diamonds in a Daisy Field* and *Legacy of Words*. I have co-authored with my husband, *Fierce Goodbye* (a book on suicide, which includes seventeen poems as well as text.) I am a professional dressmaker/designer and I enjoy opera, theater, gardening and interior decorating. Many of my poems have been put to music, won prizes and used in Christmas cards. My books may be ordered by writing to me at Lloyd.carr@gordon.edu.

Rebekah Crain – I have been a runner for fifteen years. I have wanted to be a writer since I learned how to string words together on paper. People inspire me; I believe each person has a unique and fascinating story. After graduating with a BA in English, I went into the military on active duty. I thought with exposure to new places and people I would find better, richer stories over time. Now I work for Minerals Revenue Management, and am a mother of a fiercely independent little girl. I am also a member of the National Association of Professional Women.

William (Bill) Creed began his writing career as a teenager when he approached a local newspaper editor with the idea of writing a weekly column for teens. While in the Air Force living in Germany, Bill penned a guide for servicemen entitled, *G.I. in Germany*. After his discharge, he spent the next 20 years producing and promoting concerts and other entertainment events with such artists as Dottie West, Little Jimmy Dickens, Box Car Willie and many others. A talented singer himself, Bill also recorded his own songs in the mid-1980s. Since 1998, he has written three critically-acclaimed books, *Comes the End, The Gathering* and *The Promise*. He spends a great deal of time traveling around the country doing book signings at book stores and military installations. He currently lives in Romeo, Michigan with his wife, Sharon. Together they have five children and two spoiled dogs.

Sandra Jones Cropsey writes plays, screenplays, children's stories, and recently published her first novel, *Who's There*, which was a finalist for the 2008 "Georgia Author of the Year Awards" and ForeWord Magazine's "Book of the Year Awards." Originally written as a play, *Who's There* is being considered for production by several theaters, and an audio version of the novel is in the works. Her first children's book, *Tinker's Christmas*, was published in 2002 and sold 600 copies in four weeks. With assistance from a Grassroots Arts Program grant, a fully-dramatized abridged edition of *Tinker's Christmas* was broadcast as a radio drama on several radio stations in Georgia in 2008. To hear excerpts from *Tinker's Christmas*, please check the "Media Page" at www.sandracropsey.com. Working with musician and composer Danny Smith of Night Sky Music Studio, original music is being written for a forth-coming production as a play.

Kerri Davidson is an Indiana native who graduated with a BA in English and Dance from Otterbein College in Ohio. Upon graduation, Kerri achieved her childhood dream of moving to New York City and currently works in the publishing department of Practising Law Institute. Kerri is an active volunteer with New York Cares and a writing mentor with Girls Write Now. She has written articles for Girls Write Now's blog, newsletter, and anthology; and has read memoir and poetry pieces at several New York City venues. In her free time, she loves to dance. Kerri can be reached at 3kerri@gmail.com.

Ysabel de la Rosa's writing has been published in 40+ publications in the US, Latin America and Spain. Her poetry has appeared in *Calyx, Nimrod, Oregon East, Phoebe, Southwest American Literature, Connecticut Review, Confluence, Wisconsin Review,* and *Eclipse,* among other publications. Her work was also published in the anthologies, *Texas*

151

Poetry Calendar and *The Weight of Addition.* She is the editor of *DreamBones* by poet Shelia Campbell and was a finalist for the Pablo Neruda Award in 2006. She is a member of the Authors Guild, Academy of American Poets, and Editorial Freelancers Association. http://www.ysabeldelarosa.com   http://ysabeldelarosa.blogspot.com www.artislingua.com

Bruce Dethlefsen has three books of poetry. His latest, *Breather,* was published by Fireweed Press. Bruce is a retired educator and lives in Westfield, Wisconsin.

Karen Elvin has published *A Collection of the Therapist's Heart: Art Therapy and Spirituality.* Her expressive art works have been in juried shows through Western Pennsylvania and in the Washington D.C. area as well as a Lilly co-sponsored travel exhibit of art and healing. A television interview was held in the northeastern Ohio viewing area about her book and personal art via a show titled: *Creative Living.* An art exhibit was featured in Clearfield, PA about a "Creative Senior." While Karen's main career was in professional counseling and family therapy, her main passion is encouraging the art process for those persons in nursing homes or community health programs. In witnessing the transformation of a person of health challenge as stroke, mental illness, cancer or autism, Karen has found this most rewarding. Please reach Karen at Kelvin@sssnet.com or write to her at 1826 Lake Creek Cir, NW, Massillon, OH 44647. Karen is available for workshops, retreats or sharing her stories and art.

Susan (Willms) Fast began writing spiritual poetry and journaling as a way of healing herself from bouts of anxiety, panic attacks and low-grade depression. As an active member of the Niagara United Mennonite Church, she currently participates in their choir and support groups. At 69 years old, she has been speaking for Stonecroft ministries and their Christian Women's Clubs for the last two years. Married with two adult daughters and two granddaughters, Susan has so much more to share and would love to hear from you at - sue.butterfly@live.com or R.R.#3, 2029 Four Mile Creek Rd., Niagara-on-the-Lake, Ont. Can. L0S 1J0

Robert D. Fertig has hundreds articles/stories and six books published: two on travel, another on cancer plus three business manuals. With large, small screen and stage credits plus Hearst Sunday bi-lined columnist, advertising copywriter, Radio & TV Director/Producer, adjunct professor Golden Gate University, San Francisco. Former central board member California Writer's Club and Bay Area Travel Writer's

Club, he held several senior level corporate positions and currently teaches two classes on travel, another on etiquette. His work has appeared in *Porthole Cruise, Transitions Abroad, Marco Polo, Complete Woman, International Living, Traveller (UK), SpeciaLiving. Family Fun, Cooking, Fifty Something, Nat'l Mgmt Assoc., Not Yet Retired, Grit, Travel Times, Human Resources Bulletin, I Love Cats, Art Times, I Love Dogs, Senior Times and Senior American News.* Please visit his website at www.robertfertig.com or email him at robertfertig@yahoo.com.

Gary W. Fort began his poetry career in 1982, one of his very first poems, "Reunion" was published by Fine Arts Press. He has contributed to the following magazines, *True Confessions, Modern Bride Magazine, Class Magazine, Essence magazine, Modern Romances.* He has written and sold greeting cards to major companies, has won numerous awards, has been published in over 100 literary magazines and is a published songwriter.

Kathleen Gerard's writing has been widely published in literary journals and anthologies, as well as broadcast on National Public Radio (NPR). Her fiction was awarded the *Perillo Prize*, the *Eric Hoffer Prose Award* and was nominated for *Best New American Voices*, all national prizes in literature. "Bells and Whistles" is an excerpt from *Still Life*, a spiritual memoir. She lives in Northern New Jersey and can be reached at katgerard@aol.com

Annette Geroy – After 32 years as a teacher in public education, Annette now works extensively with women who have suffered sexual abuse. She is a lay minister with Mount Horeb House Ministries in Kerrville, TX. Her recently published book, *Looking With New Eyes, My Journey from Bondage to Freedom* examines her personal healing journey from childhood sexual abuse. It was adopted by Precept Ministries, Int'l. and has been used extensively in prison ministries. Currently working on a new book entitled *My Favorite Color is Turquoise, Learning to Walk in Freedom,* she is also a conference speaker and freelance writer. She can be reached at www.mounthorebministries.com.

Constance Gilbert is the editor of 4Him2U. As a retired nurse, an adoptive mother, and a "gramma" living in the mountains of Oregon, she is filled with inspiration for her writing. Her stories have been published in several anthologies and she's currently writing several e-books, which will be available at http://www.4Him2U.com. Connie's Coda, her monthly column on surviving emotional abuse, can be found at www.positivelyfemininee.org. She delights in mentoring other writers and desires above all else to encourage others through her written words. She can be contacted at constancegilbert@gmail.com.

Hanoch Guy, who grew up in Israel, is a bilingual poet in Hebrew and English and an Emeritus professor at Temple University. His poetry has been published in *Genre, Poetry Newsletter, Tracks, The International Journal of Genocide Studies, Visions International, Poetica* and *In Other Words*. Hanoch draws his inspiration from desert landscapes, imaginary journeys and discoveries of unique spiritual gems as Donna de la Pena.

Lyn Halpern's creative non-fiction, fiction and poetry has been published in such literary journals as *Bellevue Literary Review, Karamu, Fiction International, Snake-Nation Press Journal, Pinyon, Wreckage of Reason: An Anthology of Contemporary Women Writers* and others. In 2005, she was nominated for a Pushcart Prize by Fiction International. She is the author of *Adventures of a Suburban Mystic* and *Mystic Souls: Nineteen Remarkable People Tell Their Stories*. For many years she taught out of the Philosophy Department of Rockland Community College of SUNY and presently is with Cabrini Immigrant Services in Dobbs Ferry, NY.

Carolyn T. Johnson, a former banker and now freelance writer from Houston, Texas, draws on her colorful life experiences in the US, Europe and South Africa as sustenance for her essays and poetry. Her subject matter comes from the heart, the hurt, the heavenly and sometimes the hilarious. Life has provided many twists and turns over the years but when she gets a chance to sit it out or dance, she follows the advice of Lee Ann Womack and dances. She has been published in the *Austin American-Statesman* newspaper, *Zygote in My Coffee* and *Tower Notes* of St. Andrews Methodist Church.

Lynn C. Johnston is the founder of Whispering Angel Books and has been awarded five Editor's Choice and two President's Awards for Literary Excellence for her poetry. More than a dozen of her poems have been published in several anthologies, including *Forever Friends, Timeless Mysteries, Antiquities, The World Awaits, Turning Corners and Bridges*. Lynn's work has been featured online at Blue Turtle Crossing, The Poetic Cafe and Mirrors of Expression, reprinted in inspirational newsletters and used by therapists in grief counseling. Her poetry has also attracted poetry lovers at several California book festivals, including the Los Angeles Times Festival of Books. Originally from New York, Lynn is a graduate of SUNY New Paltz. She moved to the Los Angeles area in 1988 where she currently lives with her teenage son. For more information, please visit her website at www.lynncjohnston.com or view her poetry videos at www.youtube.com/lynnthepoet.

Julia Katz, a second year college student, loves her new puppy, Isabelle. Julia enjoys painting and writing poetry in her spare time.

Rick Kempa lives in Rock Springs, Wyoming, where he teaches writing and philosophy and directs the Honors Program at Western Wyoming College. His work appears frequently in *Bellowing Ark*, a bimonthly journal which affirms that the human condition is a hopeful one, *The Chrysalis Reader*, a contemporary journal of spiritual discovery, and *The Healing Muse*, a journal devoted to the themes of medicine, illness, disability and healing. "Nothing Dies Here" was included in *Keeping the Quiet*, a collection of his poems, published by Bellowing Ark Press in 2008. http://wiki.wyomingauthors.org/Rick-Kempa

Melissa Kesead – I am the mother of two wonderful children who constantly give me ideas and inspire me to write. I started writing when I was a child, using poetry to express myself when words alone wouldn't do. I am the author of: *Walter the Dreamer and The Pirates, Walter the Dreamer and The Parade, Walter the Dreamer in the Jungle* and *Walter the Dreamer in the Enchanted Wood*. When not writing, I enjoy fishing and lobstering at home in Key West. You can find me on: Facebook: www.facebook.com/melissa.kesead, WritersCafe: www.writerscafe.org, Authors Den: www.authorsden.com/melissakesead and my website www.melissakesead.com

Judy Kirk describes her poetry as "a bit of whimsy, a lot of heart and an occasional surprise." She began her career as an advertising copy writer, and after retirement began writing poetry. In 2007, she self-published her first chapbook, *Eclipsing the Gray*, a collection of poems about growing older. In 2008, she self-published *The Poetry of Prayer* as a fundraiser for her church. Judy has also taught copywriting and memoir writing. She is a graduate of Indiana University and lives in St. Louis Park, MN. You can reach her a lilymaepress@earthlink.net.

Edward Louis is a widower and retired executive. He is a father of three and grandfather of four. He enjoys spending time with his family, solving Sudoku puzzles and traveling via plane and cruise ship.

Born in South Boston, **Susan Mahan** has been an editor for the *South Boston Literary Gazette* since the fall of 2002. She began writing after her husband died in 1997. Poetry has been a great source of solace to her. She has published three chapbooks, *Paris Awaits, In The Wilderness of Grief* and *Missing Mum*. In addition, she has been published in numerous publications and anthologies.

Vincent F. Maher, a lawyer, political economist, clinical ethicist, registered nurse and poet, is a tenured full professor of legal studies and management in the Hagan School of Business at Iona College, NY. He has written or presented over 200 articles and papers in scholarly publications, national and international conferences on a variety of themes relating to law, ethics, economics and health policy. Vincent belongs to multiple professional societies including the NY Academy of Medicine in which he is a Fellow, and the NY State Bar Association. In his work as a published poet he has participated in workshops led by David Watts, Kim Addonizio, John Fox among others.

Olga Mancuso is an antiquarian book dealer, poet and freelance writer. She's a columnist for *The Christian Journey News* and has written for *The Homeless Voice, Teen Challenge*, and *Hearts with Hands*. Her lifetime encompasses a 20-year indulgence in Human Services with qualifications in Advocacy. She's been a devoted worker for Kids in Distress and is a member of the DBSA Speakers Bureau advocating for the Mental Health Parity Act. She's certified in: Mental Health, Nursing, Domestic Violence, HIV/AIDS, Behavior Analyst Techniques and she's a Foster Parent. Presently, Olga is forming A Not For Profit for the Deaf community, ASLplace.com

Aphrodite Matsakis, Ph.D., is a practicing counseling psychologist and the author of 13 books, five book chapters and numerous articles on trauma recovery, relationships and other psychological topics. Information about her publications and articles for download are available on www.matsakis.com. She's conducted over 50 presentations for national and international groups, had over 40 media presentations and taught at the Johns Hopkins University and the University of Maryland. She's a regular contributor to several Greek-American publications and her poetry has appeared in *Open Minds Quarterly, The Writer's Circle On Line, Moon Journal, The Greek Star, She Mom and Love's Chance Magazine.*

Barbara Mayer is a Benedictine Sister of Mount St. Scholastica in Atchison, KS. She has been a teacher, journalist, and public relations director. She enjoys writing short stories, poetry and personal essays.

Jean L. McCorkle-Kaess is a freelance writer in South Louisiana. She is an award winning poet and journalist who holds a Bachelor's degree in English with a concentration in Creative Writing from Nicholls State University in Thibodaux, LA. Most recently, her poem *A Muse Named Sally* won the Louisiana State Poetry Society's annual contest. She is a mother, daughter, wife, and friend experiencing life as a 30-something in the "sandwich" generation of life. Jean can be reached at jlmk@poetic.com.

Precious McKenzie holds a Ph.D. in English from the University of South Florida. She teaches writing and literature at the college level. Her writing and research interests focus on issues of gender, class and power. She has published poetry, short stories, children's literature and academic articles. Her recent books include *Steller Sea Lions, Whooping Cranes, Manatees*, and *Forces of Nature*. In her spare time she enjoys walking with her dogs, horseback riding, and music.

Sarah Merritt currently resides in Raleigh, North Carolina with her dog, Sadie. She has an undergraduate degree in Journalism from the University of North Carolina at Chapel Hill, and her current writing includes creative nonfiction and poetry. Posted on her blog are similar sonnets and excerpts from her memoir at http://swmerritt.blogspot.com/. Sarah's writing is inspired by her desire to express the freedom and direction she has found through her faith in God, the source of hope that is always present and available.

Tanya Miller has been teaching high school English for the last fifteen years in Park Rapids, Minnesota. She received her M.A. in English from Bemidji State University in 2004 and her M.F.A. in creative writing from Minnesota State University, Moorhead in 2005. She and her husband Richard live on a forty acre farm near Park Rapids, Minnesota, where they raise organic food. They have twin daughters, Emma and Anna. "Hope" is a chapter from a book-length memoir about infertility.

Karen M. Miner was born in Rochester, New York, the only daughter of John and Jayne Quackenbush. It is her theory that one day poetry will be discovered in our DNA. Throughout her life, in times of sorrow or bliss, death or birth, triumph or defeat, she has found solace in verse and rhyme. Her vocation is nursing (RN); through this profession she has met inspiring angels. She has co-authored two books of poetry with Robert B. Moreland entitled *Eternal not Immortal: Prayers Poems and Promises for the Journey of Life* (Trafford, 2005) and *Postcards from Baghdad: Honoring America's Heroes* (Xlibris, 2008).

Caroline Misner was born in a country that, at the time, was known as Czechoslovakia. She immigrated to Canada in the summer of 1989. Her work has appeared in numerous consumer and literary journals in Canada, the USA and the UK, including *The Windsor Review, Prairie Journal* and *Dreamcatcher*. Her short story, *Strange Fruit*, has recently been nominated for the Writers' Trust/McClelland-Steward Journey

Anthology Prize. She currently lives in Georgetown, Ontario, where she works as a jeweler and continues to read, write and follow her muse, wherever it may take her. Additional work can be viewed online at www.thewritersezine.com, www.truepoetmagazine.com and www.bewilderingstories.com.

Bob (Robert) B. Moreland has a doctorate in biochemistry and has published poems in *The South Dakota Review*, *Towards the Light* and *Rope and Wire*. He has co-authored a book of poems about facing death with Karen M. Miner entitled *Eternal not Immortal* from Trafford Publishing in 2005 and a second collaborative poetry collection with Karen entitled *Postcards from Baghdad: Honoring America's Heroes* from Xlibris/ Random House in late 2008. Bob lives on the Chiwaukee Prairie in Carol Beach near Lake Michigan in Pleasant Prairie, Wisconsin.

Sheryl L. Nelms is the author of 13 collections of poetry including, *Their Combs Turn Red In The Spring*, *The Oketo Yahoos*, *Strawberries and Rhubarb*, *Rural America*, *Land of the Blue Paloverde*, *Friday Night Desperate*, *Aunt Emma Collected Teeth*, *Secrets of the Wind*, *Howling At the Gibbous Moon* and *Greatest Hits 1978-2003*. Her work has also been published in numerous magazines, anthologies and textbooks, including *Reader's Digest*, *Modern Maturity*, *Poetry Now*, *The American Anthology* and *This Delicious Day*. Originally from Marysville, Kansas, Sheryl has edited several literary magazines and taught writing and poetry at colleges and universities around the country. She is currently a member of the National League of American Pen Women, The Society of Southwestern Authors and Trinity Writers Workshop.

Linda O'Connell, a Member of Distinction with St. Louis Writer's Guild, is an award-winning, multi-genre writer. Her inspirational prose, poetry and articles have been published in ten *Chicken Soup for the Soul* books, numerous anthologies, books, mainstream and literary magazines such as *Reader's Digest*, *Reminsce*, *Joyful Woman*, *Whispers from Heaven*, *Boomer Women Speak*, and many more. Linda has been an early childhood educator for thirty-two years. The small, simple things in life make her joyful, evening walks with her husband, Bill, unexpected visits from their children, grandchildren's hugs and dark chocolate. She can be reached at billin7@yahoo.com.

Amy S. Pacini is a freelance writer from Land O Lakes, Florida. She is a 1994 graduate of Houghton College with a B.S. in Business Administration. She is a volunteer reader for Short Poems website. She has held memberships in Poets Love, Brandon Poets & Artists Guild, The International Women's Writing Guild and The Write Time. Her work has been published in *Hanging Moss Journal, Sand, Captains of Consciousness Journal, Moondance Online* and *Creative Writing Online*. She writes poetry, short stories, personal essays, and motivational quotes. Amy owns and operates A.S.P INK and its site www.amyspacini.com

Christian novelist, blogger, and award-winning travel writer, **Perry P. Perkins** is a stay-at-home dad who lives with his wife Victoria and their two-year-old daughter Grace, in the Pacific Northwest. A student of Jerry B. Jenkins Christian Writer's Guild, his novels include *Just Past Oysterville, Shoalwater Voices*, and *The Light at the End of the Tunnel*. Perry has written for numerous Christian magazines and anthologies, and his inspirational stories have been included in twelve Chicken Soup collections as well. Examples of his published work can be found online at www.perryperkinsbooks.com, and on his Examiner page: http://tinyurl.com/l46hoy

Ed Roberts was born and raised in Oklahoma City, Oklahoma. His books include *"A Poet's Last Stand"* (2002), *"I'm Still Standing"* (2003), *"Everything Must Have a Beginning, a Middle, and an End"* (2005) which are available as an e-book from Sony.com and *"Whispers, Tears, Prayers, and Hope"* (2008), which is available from Amazon.com. He is the founder, writer, and publisher of the books that make up The Poetry For Life Project. www.thepoetryforlifeproject.com His latest book *Whispers, Tears, Prayers, and Hope* was nominated for both the Pulitzer Prize in Poetry and the Oklahoma Book Award.

Nikki Rottenberg – I am a Jewish believer living in Ontario, Canada. My profession as a registered social worker is one I find great satisfaction in, but my passion is writing. I have written articles for a local newspaper, recently came in second place in the God Uses Ink Contest for my article, *Journey of Faith* and I have been featured on *Breathe Again Magazine*, a radio program in Virginia. I am in the process of publishing my first full length book, *In the Eye of Deception*. I can be contacted at blueheron123@sympatico.ca or through my blog: www.cultofdeception.blogspot.com.

Sharon Scholl, PhD. is a retired professor of humanities from Jacksonville University (FL). Author of three poetry collections: *Unauthorized Biographies, All Points Bulletin*, and *Message on a Branch*. She has received a grant from the Witter-Bynner Foundation for Poetry for a six-part TV series on local poetry and study awards from the Fulbright Foundation and Woodrow Wilson Foundation. "I write to try to figure things out and understand more clearly what life is about."

Margie Scott is the mother of one grown son and lives in Arizona. She is disabled with Parkinson's and chronic spine conditions. She loves writing, sewing and knitting. She has written devotionals for Rest Ministries, and published several poems and short stories. My goals and desires are to write to encourage others that face chronic illnesses and loneliness. She can be reached at mscott123@cox.net, and Margie Scott on Facebook.

Joanne Seltzer was born in Detroit but has lived in upstate New York long enough to call it home. Hundreds of her poems have appeared in a variety of journals and anthologies, and she has published three small press poetry chapbooks. Some of her poems have been set to music, some used as classroom texts. She has served as a contest judge. Seltzer's first true poem, *Dreamland*, was written at the age of seven and published the next year in Children's Playmate Magazine. Her most recent poetry collection, *Women Born During Tornadoes*, was released in January 2009 by Plain View Press, an issue-based literary publishing house. For more information about this poet, please visit www.Joseltzer.com.

Frances Seymour is a published author with two books released, *The Significance of a Dream* and *Perils & Promises, Life on Mission*. A third title is coming, *Mediocrity to Maturity, A Woman's Journey through Despair and Repair*. Frances has had many articles published through newspapers and magazines. She is certified in "the school of hard knocks." She has openly shared many life experiences on talk radio. Frances writes from the heart with a deep passion for who God is and what he means in her life. You can learn more @ www.authorsden.com/fseymour or view her complete bio at www.freewebs.com/fsseymour

Elaine Dugas Shea, born in New England, misses the ocean, but loves living in Montana. Shea has enjoyed a career in social justice--working in Civil Rights and serving American Indian Tribes. Her writing was featured in *Montana Voices Anthology*, *Intermountain Woman*, *Third Wednesday* and will soon be published in *South Dakota Review* and upcoming anthologies: *The Light in Ordinary Things* and *Of a Certain Age: Voices of Experience*. Shea feels poetry is a gift from God – never planned or contemplated, but always appreciated. For fun, Elaine loves playing with her spirited grandsons Arthur and Walter.

Deb Sherrer is a writer, yoga instructor, licensed school psychologist and activist in violence prevention. She lives in Shelburne, Vermont with her husband and daughters, age 9 and 12. Her poetry has been published in *The Burlington Poetry Journal*, *The Mountain Troubadour*,

Affilia and *Violence Against Women International Journal.* More of her essays and poems can be read at: www.debsherrer.com

Naty Smith started writing at the age of 14. She was the editor of the school newspaper in both high school and college and also won first place in a school poetry contest. After college, life took over and had to place her writings on hold, but all the while she knew something was missing. So in 2009, with a plot already in her mind, she decided to pursue some of her dormant dreams by beginning to write a book. This was the missing piece to her life, and feeling alive again, promised herself that she'd never stop writing again.

Molly Tienda – I'm from Grand Prairie, Texas and have lived there most of my life. I wrote this poem about this homeless guy that walked the streets of Grand Prairie. I'm sorry to say that I haven't seen him for a few years now. I wish I could tell him that he inspired me to write this beautiful poem and that I still remember him even if his family, friends and society don't. I think of him every time I read this poem. I hope Jesus has a seat with his name on it near his throne.

Gina Troisi is a finalist for the Eric Hoffer Award for Prose. Her essays are forthcoming in *Poemmemoirstory Literary Journal*, and in *Best New Writing 2009*. A graduate of the University of Maine's Stonecoast MFA Program, she now resides in Dover, New Hampshire, where she teaches community college and tends bar in order to support her writing.

Katherine K. Walker – I am a published author of a poetry book entitled: *Songs of the Feathered Wind.* When going through a particularly difficult time in my life, I began writing poetry as an outlet and haven't stopped for a moment. I love to write and my life has been the inspiration behind my work. I have won several awards for my poetry – most recently from lukevi.com for a poem called *Hungering and Thirsting*, which won first place. The *T-Shirt* won second place in the same contest. You may read these poems at the lukevi.com site. My website also features my poetry: http://www.freewebs.com/bleep7 and I would love to have you stop by and read some of my poems. My husband and I have been married for 41 years and spent most of our lives together in Indianapolis. We currently reside in El Cajon, California. My book is available from Barnes and Noble.com or Amazon.com or by asking for it at the Barnes and Noble bookstore.

Barbara Watkins resides in Sikeston Missouri with her husband of thirty-three years, one psycho kitty named 'Mila' and her faithful, loving,

161

Boxweiler pup named 'Hooch.' In 2005, her first novella entitled, *Behind the Red Door* was released followed shortly after by her second novella, *Horns of an Innocent Soul*. July of 2009, Mythica Publishing acquired the rights to publish her collection of short stories, *Nightmares & Daydreams* as an e-book and print edition. Barbara Watkins is a member of The Heartland Writers Guild in Missouri. For more info on Mrs. Watkins or her literary contributions, please visit her web site at www.barbarawatkins.net

Michele Lee Woodard was born in Lexington, KY in May 1976. She has spent most of her time helping others who are struggling in life, and writing about those situations. After achieving her lifelong dream of enlisting in the United States Navy, she became the proud mother of two wonderful boys. She gets her writing inspirations from being a Christian wife, mother, friend and child of God. Her writing can be found under her name, Michele Lee Woodard.

Cherise Wyneken is a freelance writer who found joy late in life through writing prose and poetry. Selections of her work have appeared in a variety of journals, periodicals, and anthologies, as well as two books of poetry, two poetry chapbooks, a memoir and a novel. She is a member of the Bay Area Poets Coalition, Women's Potluck and Poetry Salon, and enjoys reading her work at various other local venues. She is the mother of four, grandmother of eight, and lives with her husband in Albany, CA. More at http://www.authorsden.com/cherisewyneken

Linda Zenone – I am the mother of three grown sons and the grandmother of four. I started out as a teenager writing stories and poems for the school newspaper. One of my English teachers wrote in my yearbook, "Linda, don't ever put down that pen." I never have. Mostly I write about little things in everyday life that inspire me and might give encouragement to others. You can visit my blog at www.blogs.myspace.com/enonez

WE WANT TO HEAR FROM YOU

Has one or more of the stories touched your heart? Has it made you think differently about your own situation? We would like to hear your thoughts or comments.

Do you have a short story or poem that you'd like to see in a future Whispering Angel Book? If so, please go to our website for upcoming book topics and submission guidelines.

Whispering Angel Books is dedicated to publishing uplifting and inspirational stories and poetry for its readers while donating a portion of its book sales to charities promoting physical, emotional and spiritual healing. We also offer fundraising programs to help you increase revenue for your charitable organization. If you'd like more information, please contact us.

To contact us or to order additional books, please visit:

www.whisperingangelbooks.com

9 780984 142101